Professional Development Schools

Combining School Improvement and Teacher Preparation

Edited by
Lucindia Chance
University of Louisiana

An NEA Professional Library Publication

The Editor

Lucindia Chance is Dean of the College of Education at the University of Louisiana in Lafayette, Louisiana. She was formerly Assistant Dean at the University of Memphis, Tennessee.

Copyright © 2000 by National Education Association of the United States

All Rights Reserved

Printing History
First Printing: June 2000

Note
The opinions expressed in this publication do not necessarily represent the policy or position of the National Education Association. Materials published by the NEA Professional Library are intended to be discussion documents for educators who are concerned with specialized interests of the profession.

This book is printed on acid-free paper. This book is printed with soy ink.

ACID FREE
∞

Library of Congress Cataloging-in-Publication Data

Professional development schools: combining school improvement and teacher preparation/editor, Lucindia Chance.
p. cm. — (NEA school restructuring series)
Includes bibliographical references (p.).
ISBN 0-8106-1869-9 (pbk.)
1. Laboratory schools—Tennessee—Memphis—Case studies.
2. Teachers—Training of—Tennessee—Memphis—Case studies.
3. School improvement programs—Tennessee—Memphis—Case studies.
4. Educational change—Tennessee—Memphis—Case studies.
I. Chance, Lucindia. II. Series
LB2154.M45 P76 2000.

CONTENTS

FOREWARD 5

PREFACE 7

CHAPTER 1: Creating a New Institution
Nate Essex, Vivian Gunn Morris,
Marty M. Harrison, Fred Johnson 9

CHAPTER 2: From Paradigm into Action
Lucindia Chance, Deborah Riley,
Lirah Sabir, Lillian Whitney 21

CHAPTER 3: A Reflective Mentoring Model
Dennie L. Smith 31

CHAPTER 4: University Liaisons: Professors Who Come To Stay
Vivian Gunn Morris, Satomi Izumi Taylor,
Marty M. Harrison, Rebecca Wasson 43

CHAPTER 5: Roles and Responsibilities of Participants
in Professional Development Schools
Robert C. Kleinsasser, Mary Jo Bird,
Sr. Jean Marie Warne 61

CHAPTER 6: A Consensus-Building Model for School Improvement
Thomas Rakes, Lucindia Chance, Bonnie Cummings,
Jane Trace, Nancy Harris, Sondra Chism 71

CHAPTER 7: Teacher Empowerment: How Does It Emerge?
Vivian Gunn Morris, John Nunnery,
Satomi Izumi Taylor, Janie Knight, Pat Brooks 93

CHAPTER 8: The Role of Evaluation
Mary Lee Hall, Lucindia Chance, Tom Rakes 115

CHAPTER 9: **Cultural Changes at the School and University**
Vivian Gunn Morris, Marty M. Harrison,
Judith N. Byrd, Dorothy Robinson 125

APPENDIX 145

ACKNOWLEDGMENTS 153

FOREWARD

In the University of Memphis PDS collaborative, the university is not in the business of "fixing the schools," nor is it perceived as remaining in its ivory tower while teachers struggle to make the transfer of theory into application. The schools are valued as the learning laboratories where theory and practice merge into application and daily problem solving. P-12 teachers are viewed as equal partners and professionals with expertise in training pre-service teachers. The results are exciting. More university faculty are involved in schools, P-12 teachers are feeling empowered and renewed while choosing to remain in classrooms, cooperative research is happening, and planned and sequenced staff development is happening in the schools and at the university. University and P-12 teachers are focused on helping pre-service teacher candidates, new, and veteran teachers grow into empowered, professionally capable, and reflective teacher-leaders who are prepared to face the challenges of today's classrooms.

The overall purpose of the University of Memphis PDS program is to improve student learning in P-12 schools through simultaneous renewal of the teacher education programs at the University and teaching and learning in P-12 schools. PDSs function as laboratory schools that are not located on a university/college campus.

This book focuses on the "how to" of developing professional development schools without external funding, the challenges of developing such a partnership, the pitfalls, and the benefits of such a model to schools and to the University. The reader is encouraged to contact any or all of the chapter writers at the University web site. Reflective of the true partnership that exists at the University, each chapter is co-authored by school and university faculty involved in PDS program implementation.

PREFACE

As Americans begin to re-examine our beliefs, behaviors, and understanding, we are finding validity in many of the "old ways." Medical science is discovering the benefits of chicken soup, sociologists are confirming those behaviors essential for social stability, and educators are recognizing the need for collaborative relationships throughout the entire education community. *Professional Development Schools: Combining School Improvement and Teacher Preparation* addresses one of the most crucial challenges of our time: the development of teachers who will teach our children during the twenty-first century.

In recent years, we in education have operated in a social isolationist mode. It was as if administrators and teachers drew imaginary lines at the schools' front doors, asking parents to leave their children and allow us to educate them. We often operated as though we could and should educate children in isolation from their parents, churches, and other social influences. Teachers within the school "specialized" and sorted children into groups who needed such specialists. Very little attention was given to the whole child and his or her educational, social, emotional, and physical needs.

Likewise, teacher preparation institutions tended to train teachers in isolation, with very little input and feedback from the schools. Like their preK-12 counterparts, professors specialized in a narrow discipline or skill area such as human growth and development, reading, mathematics, social studies, or classroom management. They assumed that if teacher education candidates received the best in theory and research from each of the narrow disciplines, these professors could help them acquire the body of knowledge and application techniques necessary to become effective teachers. Like their preK-12 peers, few teacher trainers were focusing on the complex interactions of knowledge and skills necessary to produce effective teachers.

Professional Development Schools: Combining School Improvement and Teacher Preparation was first lived and experienced by the university and school co-authors of each chapter. It is published to assist schools and universities who choose to try to train teachers in a collaborative model. The old African proverb that states "it takes a whole village to raise a child" holds true and is equally as difficult in training teacher education candidates. It takes the whole education community to produce teachers who can be effective in schools of today and the twenty-first century.

The chapters in this volume support the philosophy and beliefs inherent in professional development schools. The major belief is that university and preK-12 professionals have a shared interest in improving both schools and teachers. The universities and colleges receive the products of preK-12 schools (students entering college) and preK-12 schools receive the products of universities (teachers). The education chain will be only as strong as its weakest link.

The chapters in this volume explore the fundamental elements and institutional changes experienced by a successful university-preK-12 collaborative. Working together, the University of Memphis, Memphis City Schools, Shelby County Schools, Dyer County Schools, Catholic Dioceses of Memphis, and Jackson-Madison County Schools have started and sustained thirteen professional development schools without major external funding. This volume provides insights into the successes and shortcomings of this effort.

Chapter 1

CREATING A NEW INSTITUTION

by Nate Essex, Vivian Gunn Morris,
 Marty M. Harrison, Fred Johnson

The rationale for establishing a professional development school (PDS) rests on the premise that university and preK-12 professionals have shared interests in improving both schools and teacher education. A professional development school is a learning community where professors, teachers, administrators, and prospective teachers work together to support the initial and continuing preparation of teachers while focusing on improving teaching and learning in preK-12 classrooms (Carnegie 1986; Holmes Group 1986; Nystrand 1991; Richardson 1993).

A NEW PARTNERSHIP

Traditionally, colleges of education have had the exclusive responsibility for training student teachers as well as participating in the continuing education of inservice teachers. PreK-12 professionals have generally played the major role of improving teaching and learning in classrooms. The professional development school concept departs from tradition by including practicing preK-12 professionals as full partners with their university counterparts in the teacher education process and in the development of applied research activities in the schools. This new partnership demands that university and preK-12 professionals assume new roles. Robinson and Darling-Hammond (1994) have outlined ten characteristics of successful collaborations that are helpful guides for creating a professional development school:

1. mutual self-interest and common goals
2. mutual trust and respect
3. shared decision making
4. clear focus

5. manageable agenda
6. commitment from top leadership
7. fiscal support
8. long-term commitment
9. dynamic nature
10. information sharing and communication

The initial Holmes Group, a consortium of deans and professors from schools and colleges of education, noted that a professional development school:

> ...would provide superior opportunities for teachers and administrators to influence the development of their profession, and for university faculty to increase the professional relevance of their work, through (1) mutual deliberation on problems with student learning, and their possible solutions; (2) shared teaching in the university and schools; (3) collaborative research on the problems of educational practice; and (4) cooperative supervision of prospective teachers and administrators....(The Holmes Group 1986, p. 56)

Essential to the professional development school concept is the notion of simultaneous renewal. Teacher education programs cannot be excellent without an excellent school in which to place student teachers. Schools cannot reach excellence without teachers who have graduated from excellent preparation programs. Systemic changes in this context mean that to improve one part of the system requires that the entire system be improved. Based on this belief, close collaboration between university and public school educators is critical. The theory supporting this concept is that change requires a holistic, long-term, collaborative effort between both groups (Stoddart, Winitzky, O'Keefe 1992). Professional development schools provide an ideal framework to foster this collaboration.

The initial Holmes Group (1986) formulated six principles to guide the genesis of professional development schools:

1. Teaching and learning should promote understanding. Students must do more than complete isolated drills. They must participate in meaningful learning experiences that empower them to continue to learn for a lifetime.

2. Professional development schools should be organized as communities of learning in which democracy is practiced as well as preached.
3. *All* students should be involved in learning for more specific understanding. Professional development schools must be committed to overcoming the educational and social barriers raised by an unequal society.
4. There must be an emphasis on continued learning for teachers, teacher educators, and administrators in the professional development school.
5. Reflection and research or practice should characterize life in the professional development school. New knowledge about teaching and learning should emerge through joint production by teachers and researchers.
6. The invention of a new institution should follow if the first five principles are met. New organizational structures in both schools and universities will emerge to support the total implementation of the concept.

In recent years the focus of the Holmes Group has changed. It has expanded its agenda to include a national partnership of research universities, schools and other professional organizations. The goal of the partnership is to work collaboratively to enhance the quality of schooling and academic programs in accordance with the principles and goals of tomorrow's teachers, tomorrow's schools and tomorrow's schools of education. The partnership now involves professional development school administrators, higher education administrators, higher education teachers, community and organizational leaders, Holmes Scholars and mentors, executive directors of local partnerships or consortia and superintendents. The central mission of the Holmes Partnership is to pursue the agenda for improving schools and teacher preparation through linking colleges and universities with school districts.

The professional development school concept calls for a significant shift in pedagogy in both public schools and the university. This shift can be best characterized as one that moves from didactic, teacher-directed instruction to a more clinically based approach.

This chapter focuses on the simultaneous renewal of the teacher education program at the University of Memphis and the preK-12 schools that are part of its professional development school collaborative. Included in this discussion are a description of the major components of the professional development school program as well as significant events that marked its beginnings.

REFORM AT THE UNIVERSITY OF MEMPHIS

The College of Education at the University of Memphis has thoroughly reformed its teacher training program. Initially, the faculty engaged in a process of redefining the mission of the college. Our primary mission—determined through faculty consensus—is to prepare teachers who are competent in both theory and practice. This mission was based on the belief that the most critical problem facing society is our schools, particularly inner-city schools. We believe that competent, dedicated teachers can make a major contribution to society, thereby elevating them to the status of educational leaders. Our major theme—preparing educational leaders—served as the basis for developing our curriculum. This curriculum has been completely revised to include liberal arts, general education, and educational practice. The new curriculum also focuses on developing critical-thinking and problem-solving skills, knowledge and appreciation of student diversity, and skill in the use of technology as an instructional tool.

The redefined mission that led to these changes has been embraced by top university leaders. With their support, the college reexamined its reward structure to ensure that faculty who were working in preK-12 schools would be amply rewarded. Our merit pay system was revised to make certain that outreach efforts, particularly those involving preK-12 schools, became a significant feature and assumed a high priority in our tenure and promotion process. Additionally, college faculty who were involved in preK-12 schools received a 50 percent reduction in load and additional graduate assistant support. The college also initiated three annual awards to recognize teacher education faculty who make significant contributions to teaching, research in schools, and service to schools.

Our teacher education program has a clear identity that is reflected in its budget and in decentralized decision making and authority. The program was awarded a significant number of new faculty positions to strengthen the teacher education component.

The professional development school program is an integral part of the reform efforts in the College of Education. The university launched its professional development school program in 1992 in collaboration with two local school districts and six participating schools. By the beginning of the 1995-96 school year, the partnership had grown to include 11 schools representing five school districts in West Tennessee, with 425 preK-12 faculty and an enrollment of 7,000 children. It currently involves 15 schools.

College faculty who are actively involved with public schools view the professional development school program as top priority, in the sense that they spend the majority of their time working with preK-12 faculty and students in the actual school setting. Teaching their classes at the preK-12 site allows direct observation and interaction among teacher education students and preK-12 students and faculty; it enhances the quality of the student teachers' internship experience and promotes school improvement at both the university and public school levels. A "university liaison" (college professor) is assigned half-time (or, two professors may each be assigned one-quarter time) to each professional development school site, to serve as a resource person in planning, managing, operating, and evaluating the program at the preK-12 site. In this volume, "university liaison" is used interchangeably with the term "university supervisor," which encompasses the traditional role of university professors in supervising student teachers.

HOW OUR PROFESSIONAL DEVELOPMENT SCHOOLS WORK

Our professional development school model program has four major components: (1) supervision of practice teachers, (2) school improvement planning, (3) clinical professor training, and (4) applied research and inquiry.

Supervision of Practice Teachers

As equal partners with higher education faculty in the teacher education process, the preK-12 school faculty and staff assume the lead role in supervising and evaluating student teachers. Our goal is to cluster the maximum feasible number of student teachers in each professional development school site. PreK-12 teachers who supervise student teachers in the professional development school are called "cooperating teachers." They may also be referred to as "clinical professors" if they have completed the 51 hours of professional development school training designed by the school faculty through its school improvement plan.

School Improvement Planning

Each school is required to develop and implement a school improvement plan with goals relating to students, faculty, school administrators, central administrators, parents, and community. The planning process requires that the entire faculty and staff work together in developing the plan and setting priorities for training and implementation. (See Chapter 6.) In this model, the university liaison is responsible for facilitating the development and implementation of the school improvement plan.

Clinical Professor Training

Clinical professor training needs are identified by preK-12 faculty and staff throughout the school improvement planning process. Professionals with expertise in the identified areas provide training at the school sites. All faculty who complete the required number of hours of training (those who are cooperating teachers and those who are not) receive clinical professor certificates. They are then eligible to become adjunct professors within the College of Education if they meet other requirements (i.e., appropriate degrees). "Support teachers"—specialists in areas such as music, computers, and science—are also involved in the clinical professor training along with regular classroom teachers.

Applied Research and Inquiry

PreK-12 faculty are expected to be involved in action research and presentations with their university peers. Primary focus for research activities emerges from problems that classroom teachers wish to solve. Findings from these studies are used to improve teaching and learning in professional development school classrooms.

PROFESSIONAL DEVELOPMENT SCHOOL AT A GLANCE

Our professional development schools:
- Include preK-12 professionals as full partners with their university counterparts in the development of teacher candidates and in applied research activities in the schools.
- Provide systemic induction, mentoring, and psychological support for preservice teachers.
- Foster the conceptual change from the university as a "place" to the university as a service provider or "teaching hospital" for teacher education.

REALITY SETS IN: THE WORK BEGINS

To establish the "new institution," both preK-12 schools and their university partners must share a common vision while pursuing somewhat separate goals. This vision and mutual self-interest should be clearly understood and agreed upon as they begin. The University laid the groundwork during the 1992 spring semester, when a university representative visited each school site to explain the professional development school concept as conceptualized by the College of Education. A vote of commitment by the preK-12 school faculty followed. The work actually began during inservice week of the 1992 fall semester.

Getting Our Early Education

The initial process of "becoming" a professional development school or "becoming" a university liaison, or a clinical professor in the professional development school partnership, promised to be exciting. Most university liaisons, who were professionals with a long history of teaching in preK-12 schools, looked forward to working with preK-12 teachers on a regular basis and team teaching in preK-12 classrooms. Principals also welcomed the opportunity to employ the resources of the university (seen primarily as professors who meet inservice needs) on a regular basis. These resources were provided through the professional development school partnership at no cost to the school or school district.

It was difficult not to support the professional development school concept. School administrators found the concept not only valid, but essential to the task of renewing school faculty and facilitating more meaningful student teaching experiences. University liaisons, all of whom value being closely involved in preK-12 schools' day-to-day operations, found the concept potentially very rewarding.

In early August 1992, the professional development school was launched with formal announcements by local school superintendents and the dean of the College of Education. A media blitz greeted the newly formed partnership. It was an exciting beginning, but as with many new and innovative partnerships, it was not long before the "honeymoon period" ended. In late August 1992, university liaisons and faculty members at professional development school sites faced the utter reality that what had been agreed to on paper would require considerable hard work in the form of changes in beliefs, ongoing re-evaluation of professional and personal philosophies, and a unique commitment of time and energy.

A Year of Challenge

In the first year of the partnership, the original six university liaisons encountered widely varying reactions when they visited school sites. For example, some preK-12 faculty members complained that they had not been aware of the number of inservice hours required to participate in the professional development school partnership. Other teachers displayed their dissatisfaction by conducting loud second conversations during inservice meetings facilitated by the university liaison (Morris et al. 1994). However, at other sites, the principal, teachers, and university liaison appeared to develop an almost immediate sense of trust and rapport and proceeded to work positively toward the agreed-upon goals. One way or another, it was during the first formal meeting at the individual school sites, or soon thereafter, that participants realized they were indeed all stakeholders in a major undertaking. It would entail:

- Fifty-one hours of training to become a clinical professor
- new ways of supervising student teachers
- more responsibility for evaluation on the part of cooperating teachers

- collaborative planning, writing, and implementation of a school improvement plan
- time commitment, time commitment, time commitment

As with any change process, not all the key players were willing participants. This was understandably a time of chaos, questioning, and apprehension for many stakeholders, with emotions ranging from total fear to total excitement. Of interest was how committed many administrators, faculty, and university liaisons became in changing the traditional relationship between university teacher education programs and preK-12 schools.

Initial surveys during the first year revealed that many faculty members and administrators had no clear vision of what the professional development school program would mean for their schools and in which direction it was moving. Several university liaisons were confused regarding their roles. The only constant for many of us was that we were all moving in basically the same direction, at the same time. We all agreed that we needed to significantly improve the way we train teachers and administrators and that we could do it more effectively if we collaborated. We were certain about our goal, but details of how our goal would be reached evolved gradually as we moved closer to that goal.

There were incentives for school faculty to become cooperating teachers and, eventually, clinical professors, once the required training was completed. The clinical professor status made them "adjuncts of choice" for teaching courses in the teacher education program in the College of Education. They were informed about grant-writing opportunities, on-site graduate classes, resource professionals to assist with workshops, team teaching opportunities with university liaisons, and university teaching opportunities. (See Figure 1.1.)

Each of the six site administrators and university liaisons chose to handle the initial culture shock in different ways. In retrospect, it was handled on a site-by-site basis, based upon the leadership styles and personalities of the individual pairings of administrators and university liaisons, as well as each school's existing culture. Some pairs chose to ignore the initial confusion and chaos. Others chose to move slowly and carefully in ironing out problems and dealing with high emotions of stakeholders. Still others chose to discuss anything and everything as soon as it arose.

CONCLUSIONS

Individuals in the partnership had freedom to develop their sites in different ways. Regardless of the methods chosen, it became imperative for site administrators and university liaisons to negotiate some type of mutual understanding regarding team operations.

It appears that these early negotiations speed up and smooth out the process of becoming a professional development school. When site administrators and university liaisons agree upon—and openly communicate—a joint vision and a comfortable working relationship early in the first year, the missions of all stakeholders become more clearly focused and easier to attain.

Creating a New Institution 19

Figure 1.1
Incentives Offered to Professional Development School Faculty

AT THE SCHOOL SITE
- Release time for planning
- Release time for workshops
- Grant-writing assistance
- Faculty-designed graduate classes on site
- Team-designed curriculum
- Release time for visitation at schools
- Release time for intraschool planning
- Flexibility in scheduling

AT THE UNIVERSITY
- Demonstrating in methods classes
- Serving on task forces
- Impacting curriculum development
- Teaching undergraduate classes
- Mentoring scholarship students
- Mentoring first-year teachers
- Access to library facilities
- Access to research materials
- Access to Internet/ technology support

IN THE LARGER EDUCATIONAL COMMUNITY
- Conducting workshops for other schools
- Presenting at regional/national conferences
- Publishing with university liaisons
- Designing state curriculum models
- Collaboration on statewide grant writing
- Presentations for state inservice training
- Participation in national symposiums

REFERENCES

Carnegie Forum on Education and the Economy, Task Force on Teaching as a Profession. 1986. *A Nation Prepared: Teachers for the 21st Century.* New York: Carnegie Forum on Education and the Economy.

Holmes Group X. 1986. *Tomorrow's Teachers: A Report of the Holmes Group.* East Lansing, Mich.: Holmes Group.

Morris, V. G., J. A. Nunnery, J. Scipio, J. Knight, M. Gopalakrishnan, and R. Rinehart. 1994. *A Case Study of Teacher Empowerment in a Professional Development School.* Memphis, TN: Center for Research in Educational Policy, College of Education, University of Memphis. (Technical Report No. 940101).

Nystrand, R. O. 1991. *Professional Development Schools: Toward a New Relationship for Schools and Universities* (Trends and Issues Paper No. 3). Washington, D.C.: ERIC Clearinghouse on Teacher Education.

Robinson, S. P. and L. Darling-Hammond. 1994. "Change for Collaboration and Collaboration for Change: Transforming Teaching Through School-University Partnerships." In *Professional Development Schools: Schools for Developing a Profession* (pp. 203-219). Edited by L. Darling-Hammond. New York: Teachers College Press.

Sid W. Richardson Foundation Forum. 1993. *The Professional Development School: A Commonsense Approach to Improving Education.* Fort Worth, TX: Sid W. Richardson Foundation Forum.

Winitzky, N., T. Stoddart, and P. O'Keefe. 1992. "Great Expectations: Emergent Professional Development Schools." *Journal of Teacher Education,* 43 (1) 3-18.

Chapter 2

FROM PARADIGM INTO ACTION

by Lucindia Chance, Deborah Riley,
Lirah Sabir, Lillian Whitney

In the future we must view educational reform in a more holistic manner. That is, we must stop regarding education as consisting of unrelated parts such as preschool, K-12, higher education, and business and industry training programs. We need a new paradigm to support a holistic view of an education system that extends throughout an individual's lifetime to foster economic and social stability. This new paradigm must recognize that business, industry, and higher education depend on preschool through secondary schools for academically capable students. Likewise, preschool through higher education institutions depend on funding from a strong economic base that results from successful businesses with an educated and efficient work force.

This chapter focuses on the implementation of a new model of teacher training at the University of Memphis College of Education. The creation of the professional development school (PDS) program focused on simultaneous renewal of all academic programs in the preK-12 schools and in teacher education.

Groups inside and outside the education community have consistently reported problems of the profession and insisted on solutions. For instance, some suggest that all education institutions should become learning communities, supporting education from cradle to grave (Carter 1994). Learning communities require systemic changes that will transform school employees' roles, leading to new tenets of supervisory practice, including shared supervision, and an emphasis on instructional improvements at all levels. Nolan and Francis (1992) describe several principles supporting these new perspectives. One major change includes putting into practice the belief that teachers must seek to better understand the learning-teaching process through collaborative inquiry with other educators. This means that teachers, professors, and other members of the learning community must be, not only consumers of knowledge, but also professionals who generate knowledge about learning and teaching and are actively engaged in inquiry related to it. This belief became the cornerstone of our professional development school program at the University of Memphis.

The PDS program began in spring 1992 with negotiations between the university and the superintendent of the Memphis City Schools. These negotiations sought agreement on (1) commonly held beliefs under which all professional development schools would operate, (2) school selection procedures, and (3) an implementation plan and timetables.

GOALS AND BELIEFS

The goals and commonly held beliefs forged in spring 1992 focus on the simultaneous renewal of the two institutions. The goals of the PDS program are to:

- support student learning through exemplary programs in preK-12 schools
- include the professional staff of the schools in the pre-professional education of teachers
- support inquiry and applied research in the schools

School administrators, teacher representatives and university liaisons (university staff assigned one-half time to each PDS site) review these goals annually as they relate to their school's faculty and students. They use a structured feedback procedure to record reactions and recommend modifications, and each school system and school that is selected as a PDS site must agree to adopt these goals.

Although each PDS site is different, due to its student population, mission, and school structure, each must agree to support the following agreed upon global beliefs, which focus on improving student learning:

- All children can learn.
- Student success is the goal of all school activities.

- Students need to be challenged and need to learn to pursue and persist with difficult tasks.
- Learning is an active process.
- Parental involvement is an essential element in a child's education.
- Teachers are leaders; principals are leaders of leaders.
- The business of the district and state is not to regulate, but rather to assure that schools can operate under optimal conditions.
- Staff success (including student teachers and support staff) results from motivated and competent people working in an environment that is committed to their success, continuing growth, and development.
- Instruction must be developmentally appropriate and educationally sound.

These common beliefs must be approved by each participating school system and school prior to their consideration as a PDS site. As part of an annual PDS conference, the site staff and the university administrators and staff review these beliefs and provide feedback as to how they're being implemented.

SELECTING THE SITES

University and school leaders selected schools and university liaisons according to the following five-year plan: year one—piloting and planning; year two—six sites; year three—10 sites; year four—12-15 sites; and year five—15-20 sites.

The pilot site was the University Campus School, which is a Memphis City School located on the University campus. Here, as university and school faculty collaborated in developing and piloting student teacher evaluation procedures, putting together and implementing training modules, and gathering feedback from faculty and staff, the system-wide PDS model evolved. Lessons learned from this pilot year became the watchword for implementation elsewhere.

Full implementation began in fall 1992 with six PDS sites and grew to include 13 sites at present. The list of schools located in the Memphis-Shelby County area includes ten elementary and one middle school, one university/privately funded preschool, and one parochial high school. In addition, two PDS sites are at distant locations—one a small public county school located 100 miles from Memphis and the other an inner-city school located 85 miles from the University.

The schools represent diversity in location as well as in student population. Two school populations can be classified as suburban, six as urban, one as rural, one as private/parochial, and four as inner city. The socioeconomic school descriptors range from "white collar" to "poverty." The schools' racial mixes range from 86 percent Caucasian to 98 percent African American.

To become a PDS site, schools submitted a request for consideration to the university. After the dean and the director of teacher education arrived unannounced to get a "feel" for the school and its climate, they scheduled a visit with the school administration and one with the teaching staff to explain the professional development school concept. Each group was then asked to vote whether to apply or not for PDS status.

If both groups voted to apply, the requests were considered by the Teacher Education Advisory Committee, which is made up of university personnel from within the College of Education and other colleges, as well as preK-12 personnel. Upon approval, the committee invited a university liaison from the College of Education, who has expressed interest in school involvement and who has multiple years of experience in schools, to work one-half time in the PDS. Faculty from the College of Arts and Sciences are also involved as content supervisors who visit student teachers in each site throughout the academic year.

A TRUE COLLABORATIVE

To be successful, the professional development school involves extensive collaboration between preK-12 and university faculty, and both parties must learn to trust and respect one another. As a result, training is a required component of the process. Monthly meetings are held to involve university faculty in evaluation and staff development issues and to share ideas about what is happening in each site. The group also serves as a support group for university liaisons and as a sounding board for operational changes or policy decisions. All preK-12 faculty in each PDS site become clinical professors by completing a required 51 hour professional development program that includes instruction in reflective mentoring, clinical supervision, conferencing skills, and other areas determined through the completion of a required school improvement plan.

The workshops and training take place before and after school or on Saturdays. As part of this training, school faculty are encouraged to enroll in a three semester hour graduate course on supervising student teachers. These staff development activities must grow out of the teachers' perceived needs rather than those imposed by the university. To be a true collaborative, there can be no perception that the university is in the school to "fix" it.

All university liaisons assigned to PDS sites receive training during monthly meetings held on campus and at the PDS sites. The meetings are devoted to instruction in using snapshot evaluation (a walk-through evaluation process explained in Chapter 8), facilitating the development of school improvement plans, resources and planning for ongoing professional development, and discussions of what is happening at each site. These meetings are essential to maintaining the consistency of the concept, since no two schools are alike.

SIGNS OF PROGRESS

The PDS initiative has resulted in a new portfolio evaluation system, a new student teacher guide, a targeted clinical experience placement process, methods class scheduling, and changes in several other components of teacher preparation. Teachers from the PDS sites have been directly involved in each change, an outgrowth of their involvement on all teacher education related committees.

Transforming Teacher Placement

The current program at the College of Education involves two placements each for more than 300 student teachers each semester. Of these, approximately 100 student teachers are in PDS sites. The transformation of the entire undergraduate and graduate teacher licensure program into a professional development school concept is being phased in as part of the five-year plan. The measure of success extends beyond graduating better teachers. More (approximately an 80 percent increase) full-time university faculty are involved in schools, cooperative research is ongoing and planned, and sequenced staff development based on the school improvement plan is occurring. What's more, university and preK-12 teachers are mentoring new teachers as they complete licensure programs and become educational leaders and activists.

Expanding Roles

Other signs of progress are evident in the roles played by university and preK-12 faculty. Inservice teachers are taking on new roles as they:

- conduct more school-based action research and write up their findings
- present professional papers with their higher education peers
- serve as gatekeepers of the profession

At the same time, university faculty have expanded their roles to include:

- team teaching with their preK-12 peers
- conducting collaborative research in the schools
- providing sequenced staff development based on the school improvement plan
- serving as permanent members of the school improvement team
- interacting daily with children and teachers in schools
- participating in three-way team teaching experiences with the cooperating teacher and student teacher at a PDS site or at the university.

Nurturing Teachers

Institutionalizing the professional development school concept requires nurturing school and university personnel through a mixture of activities, rewards, and empowerment type experiences. Assuming ownership means being willing to participate, "talk-it-up" and reflect a general attitude of mutual support and pride among peers. New teachers must leave their PDS experience with a sense of professionalism and sincere desire to make a positive difference in schools. Several ongoing experiences are necessary to build student teachers' professional pride and confidence and to help university and preK-12 faculty improve their own interactions with student teachers. These include training, annual PDS conferences, school visitations by teachers to other professional development schools, initiating a clinical professor program, and enabling action research to occur in schools.

Teachers in the PDS sites need support and benefits, since they are being asked to commit many hours of time in addition to their regular duties. Some of the "perks" include (1) the title of clinical professor; (2) visitation days to other PDS sites; (3) participation in PDS conferences; (4) participation at national conferences; (5) receiving faculty perks such as discounted athletic tickets, library access, etc.; and (6) a feeling of empowerment.

Clinical professors are given priority to teach at the university when adjunct faculty are selected for evening, weekend, and summer teaching. They receive pay as regular adjunct faculty since they are working at times other than during regular school hours. A priority is also given to PDS sites for scheduling undergraduate methods classes or graduate classes for inservice teachers at the site.

Greater Professionalism

Each year, several classroom teachers from professional development schools look forward to participating in half or whole day visitations in one or two other PDS sites. Such activity benefits both the visiting staff while providing an opportunity for the host staff to "show off" what they are doing. For instance, one PDS site is heavily involved in a whole language philosophy while another is implementing the middle school concept to replace the junior high model, and another has begun a mentoring program for all students in grades four through six. Teachers are enthusiastic about seeing the variety of innovations going on in different professional development schools.

In addition to an annual PDS conference held on the university campus, school faculty receive support to attend national conferences, such as the annual NEA symposium and others that help them implement their school improvement plans. Presenting research at national conferences with university peers adds prestige to the teacher's role and reinforces the importance of teachers participating in action research in preK-12 classrooms.

CONCLUSIONS

Participating in a professional development school requires collaboration between and adjustment by both university faculty and preK-12 teachers. Developing shared vision, collegiality, and respect for one another takes time and a willingness to change. Key factors in the success of the model at Memphis include: (1) "self-selection" by the schools, (2) voluntary participation of the university liaisons, (3) a true partnership which erased the previous perception of levels of importance, (4) financial and philosophical support from the university and school communities to implement and sustain achievement at all levels, (5) a shared belief that achievement at all levels is improved by external funding and collabaration. As a result of these changes, the PDS initiative is making a difference in Memphis City, Shelby, Dyer, and Jackson-Madison County school systems, and the University of Memphis. Traditional roles in these institutions are a thing of the past. One teacher expressed it best as she was signing the official recommendation for a teacher candidate's license—"Our professional development schools really empower teachers."

REFERENCES

Carter, G. 1994. "Supervision in a learning community." In *Supervision: New Roles for All. Wisconsin Association for Supervision and Curriculum Development* (p. 83). Edited by C. Heideman. Madison, Wisc.: WASCD.

Nolan, J. and P. Francis. 1992. "Changing Perspectives in Curriculum and Instruction." In *Supervision in Transition: 1992 Yearbook of the Association for Supervision and Curriculum Development* (p. 22). Edited by C. Glickman. Alexandria Va.: ASCD.

Chapter 3

A REFLECTIVE MENTORING MODEL

by Dennie L. Smith

I have developed a reflective mentoring model to guide the professional evolution of student teachers in a new and different way. When first piloted, this model represented a change in long-standing routines, attitudes, and perspectives. Applied to professional development schools, the model requires that the roles of university liaison, cooperating teacher, principal, and student teacher be re-examined for ways of providing more interactive, cooperative, and constructivist experiences.

Traditionally, while learning how to teach, student teachers have carried out their theoretical philosophies from the university under the tutorage of the university liaison and cooperating teacher. The reflective mentoring model shifts the responsibility for making classroom decisions to the student teacher, under the guidance of the cooperating teacher. Student teachers have an opportunity to "do things their way" after serious inquiry and discussion with the cooperating teacher. Both parties commit themselves to continuous learning by focusing on the instructional opportunities and challenges in meeting the needs of preK-12 students.

Many complex interactions take place among the professionals who prepare student teachers. The reflective mentoring model can serve as the framework to guide the cooperative inquiry and learning process of all who are seeking better ways to develop learning and teaching excellence. This chapter explains the various phases of the model, explores typical problems encountered by student teachers, and offers a training plan for implementing the model.

PILOTING THE MODEL

The first professional development school site—the Campus Elementary School at the University of Memphis—is a university laboratory school comprised of grades 1-6, jointly administered by the College of Education and Memphis City Schools. The support of key administrators—including a forward-looking Dean of the College of Education and an enthusiastic principal—was critical to implementing the reflective mentoring model here. Teachers at the school first attended a brief presentation describing the model, which included a description of how their roles would need to change and what training would be provided throughout the year. Although many of the teachers were very willing to work as individuals with student teachers, we felt that to make a more systemic change, the whole school must make a commitment to both the development of student teachers and the improvement of inservice training. The staff accepted the challenge.

A fundamental feature of the reflective mentoring model is that more responsibility for the student teacher's development and evaluation is handled at the school level rather than at the university. The university provides expertise in training and facilitates problem solving, if needed, but in the final analysis, the school's organizational structure is used to resolve issues and problems related to the student teacher via the reflective mentoring model. If a problem cannot be resolved at the teacher level, the principal becomes active in the process; if there continues to be little progress, the principal may invite the university liaison to join in the process. Thus, the "game" students often feel they must play in trying to please both the university and school is eliminated. Accountability is truly at the school level, with the university serving in a support and resource capacity throughout the induction process.

Greater autonomy in working with student teachers was an appealing aspect of the invitation for teachers to participate in the pilot of the model, as were the opportunities to form a closer partnership with the university and to receive training. Another factor (subtle but nonetheless powerful) was that teachers had a choice as to whether to participate in making this decision. Involving teachers in decisions that directly affect them, such as whether to participate in the model, was the first step in establishing a foundation upon which to build. The teachers believed this decision would be a model for future decisions at various levels in the classroom or at the school level, and their "buy in" was important for the implementation of the model. Both cooperating teachers and student teachers knew they would be asked to refine the model during the pilot program, and they looked forward to contributing what they learned.

The Reflective Mentoring Process

The reflective mentoring model (see Figure 3.1) provides the framework for a core process—the reflective mentoring process—by which the cooperating teacher, the student teacher, the principal and the university liaison can guide dialogue for effective decision making. This reflective mentoring process is based on the premise that teachers can reflect on their own problems, can work to solve them, and—by doing so—construct a more relevant knowledge base. Thus, the core

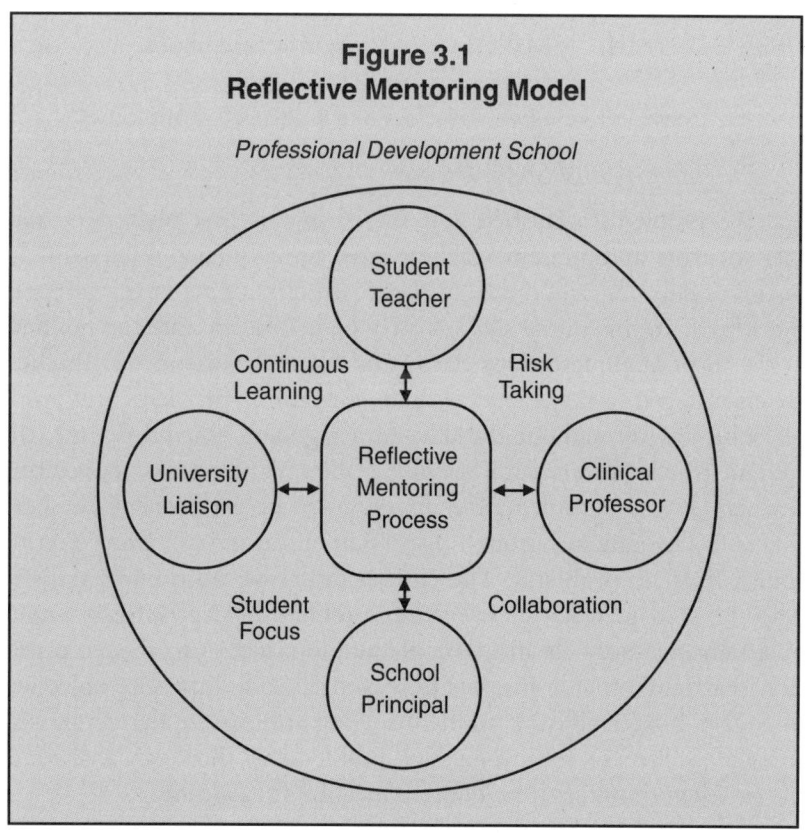

Figure 3.1
Reflective Mentoring Model

of the model becomes the encouragement of reflective and analytical thought: thinking about successes and problems and learning from these experiences in context-specific environments.

For example, as schools think about the effectiveness of cooperative learning strategies, decisions can be based on "hard data" with respect to achievement, rather than on doing what is socially or politically expedient in the school. Decisions are based both on research and experiential data and involve planned and purposeful interactions with other professionals. Although the process can be used by individual teachers or in traditional student teacher seminars, it becomes more powerful when context and professionals are involved in developing specific, alternative solutions to real problems.

The reflective mentoring process (see Figure 3.2) includes the following main components:

> Phase I: Identify and share problems
> Phase II: Share alternative solutions
> Phase III: Make a rational decision and choose a course of action
> Phase IV: Own successes and unexpected outcomes

Phase I: Identify and Share Problems

Problems identified and shared in this first phase are those that mentors and student teachers have actually encountered in the instructional program, either in their own classrooms or elsewhere in the school. In this initial stage, it may be helpful to state the problem in the form of a question to clarify and focus the discussion. Teachers are encouraged to make journal notes concerning problems and possible solutions throughout the day. At a regularly scheduled time, the student teacher meets with his or her clinical professor (cooperating teacher) to pose problems for discussion. The experienced teacher's role is to facilitate a thorough discussion and to refrain from offering "quick fixes" to problems. The clinical professor can use questions to help the student teacher explore the problem in depth, for example, by asking for more clarification, elaboration, facts, or other information that may provide insights on potential solutions. The objective, of course, is to establish a problem-solving atmosphere that empowers student teachers to solve their own problems. A thorough analysis of the problem should help to develop meaningful solutions.

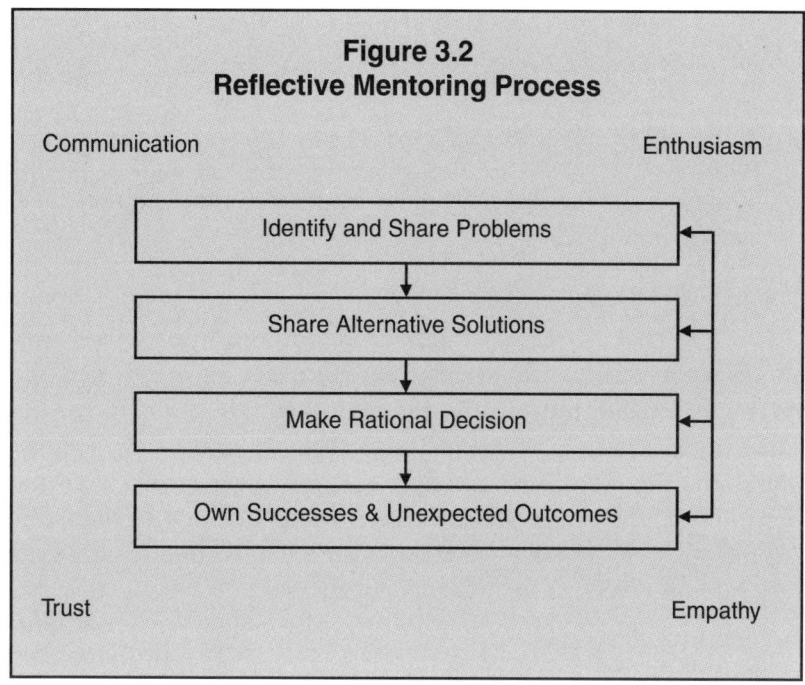

Following are examples of problems identified by student teachers:

1. How is whole language implemented in an actual classroom?
2. What are some ways of gaining students' attention?
3. What should be the main points of discussion with a parent whose child is supposedly having bad dreams from stories in the reading book?
4. Do I treat my resource students in the same manner as other students?
5. How do you handle a child who talks back to you?
6. Why did my students fail to do well on a test?
7. How do I incorporate more activity-based features in lessons?
8. How can I manage students who are disrupting other students trying to work?
9. How can various learning needs be met in widely diverse groups?
10. How can students be kept on task during discussions?
11. Why do students fail to follow directions?
12. What are some alternative ways for managing students?

13. What can be done to get students to think and try out problems before raising their hands for help?
14. How can social studies be incorporated into a science unit?
15. What can be done about a student's lack of control in the classroom?
16. What are some creative things for students to do when they finish assignments quickly?

Phase II: Share Alternative Solutions

Typically, there are a number of solutions to any given problem. Teachers must consider many variables and make a professional judgment in determining the most appropriate solution for any instructional or school problem. The complexity of the classroom and school environment is reflected in age, sex, interest, need, ethnic, social, and family issues. Furthermore, the availability of both time and instructional resources, and the existence of school requirements, must be considered in making workable decisions.

The clinical professor facilitates the generation of solutions by listening to and encouraging the flow of ideas. Brainstorming techniques can be helpful in this process. Writing down all ideas and providing some "think time" before generating solutions can also be useful.

Phase III: Make a Rational Decision

The final selection of the "best" alternative for any problem should ultimately be the student teacher's, although the clinical professor will have input through discussion during the first two phases. Moreover, the clinical teacher's interaction throughout the early stages of the process ensures that the alternative selected is based on a thought-and-conflict resolution process that carefully analyzes all the information available. Identifying factual information in the context of value-laden issues is an important part of reviewing information. In this phase, as in previous ones, probing questions can be useful in helping to analyze the problem and then make a rational decision. Each alternative should be analyzed by discussing all relevant facts and information and then determining the "pluses" and "minuses" in a summary-type approach.

Alternatives	pluses	minuses
1.		
2.		
3.		

This part of the process may take considerable time, but the end result should be well worth the effort. A carefully considered decision has more chance for success. Full support should be given to the student teacher in implementing the solution.

Phase IV: Own Successes and Unexpected Outcomes

The reflective mentoring process encourages student teachers to celebrate their successes and to own unexpected outcomes. The underlying premise in this phase is that there are no mistakes unless you quit trying. Once a solution has been selected for implementation, the problem is either resolved or there is an unexpected outcome. If the problem is resolved, a pat on the back or other acknowledgment of the good feelings that accompany success should be shared with other teachers. Most importantly, the clinical teacher should congratulate or acknowledge the success in some manner. A short note in the mail box or informal comments to other teachers may help to promote a positive and supportive environment. The ultimate reward is helping student teachers move toward increased confidence with their learning. Nothing is more contagious in a classroom than student success, and the same is true for teacher success in a school. Enthusiasm is a factor closely related to effective teaching and established through a series of successes.

On the other hand, there may be an unexpected outcome—that is, the alternative did not solve the problem. An unexpected outcome simply poses a different set of circumstances for more problem solving. Failures are those problems for which we give up trying to find new solutions. Perseverance is especially important in unexpected outcomes as teachers return to Phase III to develop alternative solutions. These solutions must now be reconsidered in light of experience. Of most importance, unexpected outcomes can be discouraging for new teachers, especially if support is not available from the clinical teacher and other school and university personnel. Prudent risk taking is encouraged throughout the entire problem-solving process.

Of critical importance to the reflective mentoring process is the amount and quality of communication existing in the school environment. Communication channels must remain open among student and cooperating teachers, principals, and university liaisons so that all can initiate conversation and exchange information freely. The ability to hear and articulate the main points in problem-solving conversation is fundamental to establishing a collegial environment. Good facilitation skills that encourage listening for understanding and for capturing the meaning of the message are essential to the success of the reflective mentoring process.

Using the Model

There are several important logistical concerns in using the reflective mentoring process. The following ground rules should be considered for establishing working agreements and expectations.

1. A daily (15-20 minute) conference should be scheduled for the clinical teacher and student teacher. The meeting should be treated as one of the most important events of the day, since clinical teachers and student teachers often interact constantly and may not perceive the need for this meeting.
2. The location for the meeting should be free from distractions. (This may be a challenge in some school environments.)
3. Participants should be prepared from notes to discuss both successes and unexpected outcomes at the meeting. Such written preparation is evidence of prior reflection.
4. Brief notes should be taken at the meeting to indicate actions. An outline of the reflective mentoring process might be visually displayed to help guide discussion and ensure the effective use of time.
5. Student teachers should maintain a journal to reflect on their own professional growth as well as their positive impact on student learning.

Training for Reflective Mentoring

Training is an essential component for successful use of the reflective mentoring model. While the model is logical and reasonable on paper, it can have many interpretations without some commonality established through training. Training should occur throughout the year both to refine the model and to develop successful skills for using the process. All teachers, the principal, and the university liaison should participate in the training. The university liaison helps to organize, and often conducts, the one-to-two-hour training sessions. Many schools establish their training agenda early in the year through a professional development planning process.

A suggested outline for the training is as follows:

1. Rationale for using the reflective mentoring model
    a. Professional environment of collegiality
    b. Mentoring relationships
    c. Professional problem solvers
    d. Common model for dialogue
    e. Change and innovation
2. Explanation of the main components of the reflective mentoring process
    a. Identify and share the problem
    b. Share alternative solutions
    c. Make rational decision
    d. Own successes and unexpected outcomes
3. Demonstration of the model
    Simulation: (e.g., problem—more accessibility to library)
4. Explanation of logistics
    a. Meeting time and place
    b. Notes to record actions
5. Role-playing the use of the model (Small Groups)
    Topic 1: Using more high level questions
    Topic 2: Teachers select real problem and try out the model
6. Developing facilitation skills
    a. Encouraging expression
    b. Clarifying terms
    c. Paraphrasing
    d. Using and responding to nonverbal clues
7. Effective communication skills
    a. Listening for understanding
    b. Speaking directly and clearly
8. Refining the model
    a. Successes in use of the model
    b. Refinement of the model

CONCLUSIONS

Some of the factors contributing to the success of the reflective mentoring model relate to other innovative practices in schools. The initial and ongoing support of the school principal is invaluable for establishing a proper environment. The opportunity to become a professional development school site can be a strong motivating factor, in that it provides additional resources from the collaborating university as well as special status within the school system. Teachers should make a sincere commitment to participate in the model and their training sessions need to involve them actively through role playing and other interactive discussions. Commitment to the model also means that time will be needed to share successes and celebrate with each other. Written documentation provides the discipline, structure, and content for the weekly meetings and will reflect the degree to which participants actually use the model. Use of the model may expand to guide other initiatives in establishing a shared language and common understanding among new and veteran professionals.

REFERENCES

Daloz, L. A. 1999. *Mentor: Guiding the Journey of Adult Learners.* San Francisco: Jossey Bass.

Fraser, J. 1998. *Teacher to Teacher: A Guidebook for Effective Mentoring.* Portsmouth: Heinemann.

Furlong, J. 1995. *Mentoring Student Teachers: The Growth of Professional Knowledge.* New York: Routledge.

Henderson, J. G. 1992. *Reflective Teaching: Becoming an Inquiring Educator.* New York: Macmillan Publishing Company.

Newman, D. R. 1996. *Reflective Teaching.* Paramus, N.J.: Prentice Hall.

Schubert, W. H. and W. C. Ayers. 1992. *Teacher Lore: Learning from Our Own Experience.* White Plains, N.Y.: Longman.

Taggart, G. L. 1998. *Promoting Reflective Thinking in Teachers: 44 Action Strategies.* Thousand Oaks, Calif.: Corwin Press.

Chapter 4

UNIVERSITY LIAISONS: PROFESSORS WHO COME TO STAY

by Vivian Gunn Morris, Satomi Izumi Taylor,
Marty M. Harrison, Rebecca Wasson

The university professor is often perceived by preK-12 professionals as someone who visits their school to collect data or give a one-shot workshop presentation and is never to be seen again until the next inservice day. But university liaisons who work in professional development schools are professors who have come to stay. The university liaison makes a long-term commitment (three-to-five years) to improving the teacher education program at the university and teaching and learning in preK-12 schools. Professional development schools provide many opportunities for professors to live in both of these worlds—and they must—if we are to significantly improve the way we prepare future teachers and administrators. University professors who are teacher educators "need to be involved in schools on a regular basis if their teaching and research are to be rooted in the realities of contemporary schooling and influenced by the views and needs of practitioners" (Richardson Foundation 1992, p. 17).

The role of the university liaison in a professional development school may vary, depending on whether the focus is on preservice teachers, inservice teachers, or both. Jones (1993) has defined three roles that staff developers, who are often university professors, play in teacher growth or educational reform efforts:

1. Storytellers, usually *experienced teachers,* seek to develop *facilitative* personal relationships and build collegiality between themselves and teachers. We have chosen to call this role *storyteller* because of the importance of observation and reflection as

facilitative behaviors and to contrast this role with the two roles we have observed in other situations, *fixer-upper* and *star*.

2. Fixer-uppers know what ought to be done and typically use suitable reinforcements to try to get it done. Fixer-uppers are most effective if they have power within the system as an administrator or supervisor or exert other coercive power as a representative of a regulatory agency.

3. Stars are charismatic experts. They are very good at what they do and excited by the doing; their hope is to inspire others to do the same (pp. xvii-xviii).

Using Jones' definition of roles, the storyteller/facilitator role may be best suited to the university liaison in a professional development school, where the priority is teacher growth that ultimately exhibits itself in improved student learning. The storyteller/facilitator looks for knowledge that teachers are already using and reflects it back to them, making teachers' own stories the starting point for learning. The storyteller/facilitator concentrates on strengths rather than weaknesses and is oriented toward teacher decision making, risk taking, divergent thinking, self observation, and reflection on practice (Jones 1993).

This chapter describes: the roles and characteristics of university liaisons, the processes of preK-12 professionals and university liaison team building, strategies for overcoming university peers' perceptions of the value of working in preK-12 schools, and lessons learned about the roles and effective functioning of university liaisons based on experiences and research findings.

ROLES AND CHARACTERISTICS OF UNIVERSITY LIAISONS

The university liaison is a College of Education faculty member who is assigned one-quarter to one-half time to work at a single professional development school site. (With large clusters of student teachers assigned to a school building, two university faculty members may be assigned to a school to form a liaison team.) This university faculty member serves as a resource person in planning, managing, operating, and evaluating the professional development school program.

Seven Tasks

Specific roles outlined in the concept paper that guided implementation of our professional development school program indicated that the university liaison would complete the following tasks (Chance 1992):

1. Assist in the development and implementation of the school improvement plan.
2. Serve as liaison between the school and the university (practice and research).
3. Train cooperating teachers in the process of evaluation, observation, reflective mentoring, and clinical supervision.
4. Establish continuity between induction (preservice) and inservice staff development programs.
5. Serve on the supervision/evaluation team for preservice teachers in the professional development school.
6. Include schools and school practitioners in action research and presentations of research findings.
7. Respectfully recognize the professional development schools as the "teaching hospitals" for the education profession.

In the first year of the professional development school, the university searched for professors to become liaisons who: (1) had a demonstrated track record of working with preK-12 professionals; (2) desired to be directly involved in the schools; (3) were enthusiastic; (4) were interested in making changes in schools in collaboration with practitioners—rather than being an expert or fixer-upper; and (5) would not give up easily. As it turned out, of the six first-year liaisons, five were junior faculty members, one was tenured, and four were new to the university faculty. Several tenured faculty members agreed to become liaisons in year three of the program and have continued in that role. Over time, more tenure-track faculty at upper ranks (associate and full professors) have taken on the role of university liaison. Faculty members from the COE Departments of Leadership, Special Education, and Human Movement and Science Education have become liaisons. In the first years of the project, all liaisons were faculty members in the Department of Instruction and Curriculum Leadership.

Liaisons were assigned 10-15 student teachers. The seven tasks noted above provided the framework for the liaison's work, but each school refined those roles, based on needs identified in the school improvement plan. Figure 4.1 represents an attempt by the liaisons to further refine their duties, based on two years of experience with individual professional development schools, as well as the tasks and roles

Figure 4.1
Description of the Duties of University Liaisons In a Professional Development School Partnership

DUTIES OF UNIVERSITY LIAISONS

Student Teachers

- Meet with student teachers on a regular basis, beginning with an initial orientation meeting, then once per week to reflect on classroom experiences.
- Make weekly observation/supervision visits to classrooms.
- Participate in two-three evaluation conferences with the student teacher and cooperating teacher (number depends on length of placement).
- Submit student teacher portfolio to Teacher Education Office at completion of placement.

Inservice Teachers

- Conduct weekly meetings with cooperating teachers.
- Facilitate the development or update of school improvement plan.
- Support and assist teachers in meeting needs identified in school improvement plans. Examples may include:
  - conducting workshops
  - finding resource people; supporting scholarly inquiry in research and grant writing
  - attending faculty meetings and PTA functions
  - re-examining needs at the beginning of the year and evaluating accomplishments at the end of the year.

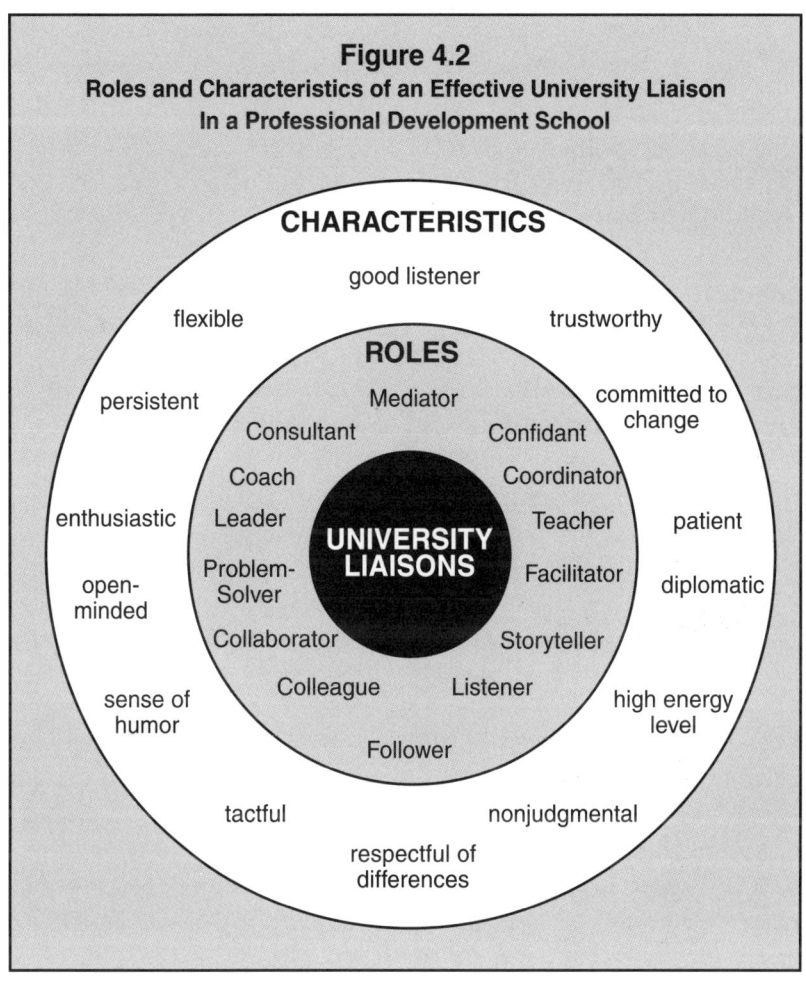

Figure 4.2
Roles and Characteristics of an Effective University Liaison In a Professional Development School

identified in the original concept paper. This list of duties may be helpful in communicating the work of the university liaison as more professors are recruited for new professional development schools, or to replace liaisons who have changed jobs or retired. This initial description may also be helpful in describing the liaisons' work to preK-12 professionals and as a basis for evaluation of tenure and promotion at the university.

Figure 4.2 describes some of the group roles that liaisons must play in order for their professional development school to be effective. It also points to some of the personal characteristics that enable liaisons to be credible agents of change. These group roles and personal characteristics are reflected in the discussions found in the next two sections on team building and overcoming the perceptions of university peers.

TEAM BUILDING BETWEEN SCHOOL AND UNIVERSITY

Many preK-12 classroom teachers believe that university professors regard themselves as higher status professionals; that is, they are "experts" who have come to tell teachers how to "fix" the problems in their classrooms and schools. Far too many college professors have earned this reputation because they are so "accustomed to 'professing' their knowledge—telling rather than listening" (Creaser 1993, p. 114). This feeling was communicated by a classroom teacher in a statement to a university liaison in a professional development school:

> You treat us as peers. There are some university people who feel that they are up there and we are down here. They (university professors) need us for their work. We don't need them (Morris et al. 1994, p. 28).

Because of this perception, many preK-12 professionals refuse to believe that the university liaison really wants to listen and that the real agenda for change will come from the classroom teachers. It requires time and patience on the part of the liaison to build rapport and trust among practitioners in professional development schools. The preK-12 practitioner must believe that the liaison has made a long term commitment to the school and that the work of the professional development school is not another short-term, passing educational fad. Our experience indicated that by the end of the first year, liaisons were accepted by most faculty members and administrators as colleagues and members of the school faculty.

Setting the Tone

The relationship that develops between the school principal or director and the university liaison is critical to the successful implementation of a professional development school. The principal must be convinced that the professional development school is a community of learners with its primary goal the intellectual development of all its members—students, teachers, administrators, professors, and future educators (Richardson Foundation 1992). It is important that the principal and the liaison begin their relationship "on the right foot" with an open and honest dialogue about the work of the professional development school and the role of the liaison in its implementation. This is an important opportunity for the liaison to reinforce the partnership/learner role versus the "expert" role of the university representative—remembering also that the work of the professional development school takes place on the turf of preK-12 professionals. This initial building of trust and rapport between these two professionals sets the stage for later roles that the liaison may play. The relationship that develops between the principal and the university liaison also sets the tone for the university liaison to establish appropriate relationships with classroom teachers and support staff.

Activities that Promote Collegiality

When it comes to building a collegial partnership between classroom teachers and university liaisons, two opportunities present themselves: school improvement planning and supervision of student teachers. As facilitator in developing the school improvement plan, the university liaison is viewed by preK-12 teachers as a listener, collaborator, follower, consultant, mediator, and problem solver. During the many hours of developing and updating school improvement action plans, the liaison's commitment to teaching and learning in preK-12 schools will be clearly evident. Add to that commitment such personal characteristics as flexibility, enthusiasm, patience, open mindedness, commitment to change, a sense of humor—and, of course, the high energy level that is required for this labor intensive work.

The relationships were strengthened as classroom teachers and liaisons worked together to implement school improvement plans. The liaison often played the roles of listener, colleague, and collaborator as the partners worked together to develop activities, programs, grants, and action-research projects to support the school improvement plan.

In supervising student teachers, preK-12 professionals (cooperating teachers) become equal partners with their higher education counterparts (university liaisons) in the university's teacher education program. To prepare them for this important work, cooperating teachers were trained by the university liaison and other university professors in the processes of evaluation, observation, reflective mentoring, and clinical supervision, in addition to undergoing the standard orientation session. This training was included as part of the 51 hours of training required to become a clinical professor during the initial years of the program.

One goal of the professional development school model is to have cooperating teachers assume the lead role in the supervision and evaluation team. In a report of one case study (Morris et al. 1994), teachers felt uncomfortable, initially, in taking the lead role in evaluation conferences with student teachers. But, by the end of the first year of the program, cooperating teachers more readily accepted the lead responsibility. They began to come to the evaluation conferences with their notes ready, sat at the head of the table, and started the conference. One teacher's response to this process was:

> Before, [before professional development school] it was more hands-off, and the professor was the total evaluator. It is impossible for a professor to be able to spend enough time to know whether the student can handle all types of situations. But the teacher is there always to offer advice and be there for him or her (p. 13).

During weekly meetings, the cooperating teachers and liaisons reflected on the experiences, strengths and needs of their student teachers. Cooperating teachers also expressed their concerns and made suggestions to improve not only the experiences of the student teaching program at the university, but other aspects of the teacher education program, such as clinical experiences prior to student teaching, course content, and classroom management skills. Figure 3 diagrams the collaborative relationship of preK-12 professionals and university liaisons that is a goal of our professional development school model.

University liaisons had further opportunities to build positive relationships with teachers, students, and parents by teaching in preK-12 classrooms as team members, along with cooperating and student teachers. By the end of the first year, liaisons had opportunities to teach classes when invited by the teacher. This was significant evidence that teachers were beginning to build a trusting relationship with liaisons. They saw that the liaisons were "real" teachers who could teach children as well as adults. Support staff, children, and parents also began to accept liaisons as members of the school community after seeing them teaching in classrooms, eating in the school cafeteria, and attending parent-teacher functions at the school. For the liaisons, some of the most fruitful sessions with classroom teachers (in terms of building collegial relationships) took place while eating in the cafeteria or during conversations in the classroom as student teachers taught and managed classroom experiences. Students often asked liaisons when they would return to teach in their classes.

Classroom teachers also had opportunities to build collegial relationships with university liaisons who were assigned to other schools in the professional development school partnership. This took place as liaisons led inservice meetings at schools other than their assigned school, as selected monthly meetings for the liaisons were held at school sites instead of at the university, and as representatives from each professional development school worked with university liaisons to develop a grant proposal that would benefit all professional development schools in the partnership. An advisory council for the partnership with representatives from each school could serve a similar

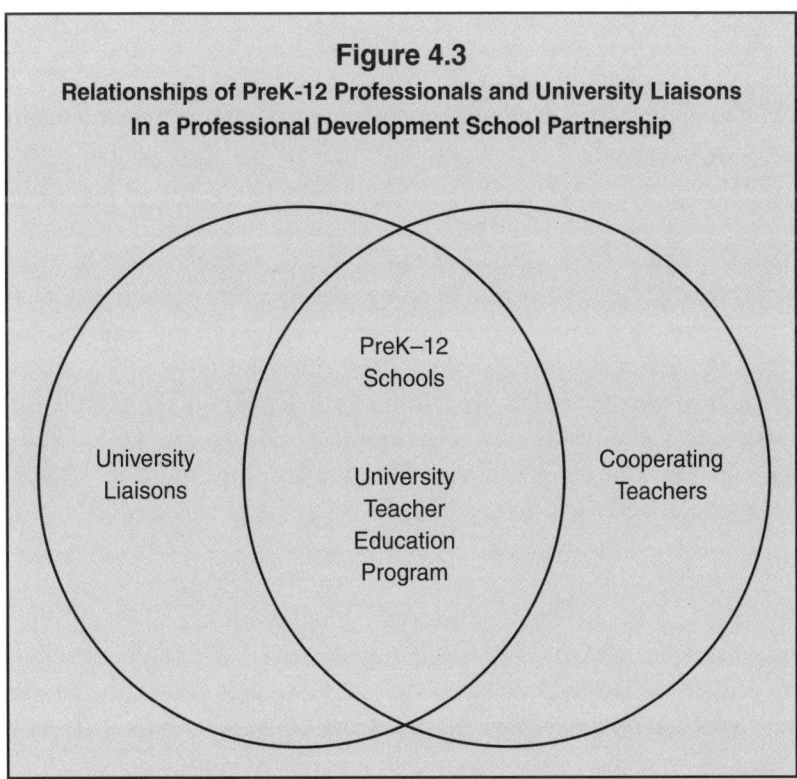

Figure 4.3
Relationships of PreK-12 Professionals and University Liaisons In a Professional Development School Partnership

function in a more consistent, ongoing fashion. A PDS advisory committee was established during the 1995-96 academic year which includes representatives from each school district and the university—classroom teachers, administrators, and teacher eductors.

VALUING WORK IN THE SCHOOLS

The pinnacle of the academy for many educators is to attain the rank of full professor in a major research university. And the way to get there in most colleges and universities is to generate new knowledge by conducting research, to make presentations at national professional conferences, and to publish, publish, publish! Probably, most teacher educators were once preK-12 teachers and many have no desire or intention to return to work in classrooms inhabited by young children and adolescents. Yet, if colleges and universities are going to significantly improve the way they prepare preK-12 professionals, teacher educators must live in both worlds so that they can build on the contemporary realities that children and practitioners bring to their teaching, research, and writing.

University liaisons in professional development schools have fresh, experientially based ideas to bring to their university methods classes because of their ongoing teaching experiences with schoolchildren and their current work with teachers, administrators, parents, and other community members. For example, one university liaison, who taught a language and methods course on campus, communicated to her students how whole language instruction was being implemented at her professional development school site. The university students also had opportunities to observe and participate in the elementary classrooms at the professional development school site. The following semester, the course was moved on-site to the professional development school, and the university students participated in a wide variety of clinical experiences related to course content. Another liaison, who taught a school/community relations course for elementary and early childhood education majors, was able to talk with her students about parent involvement activities at her professional development school site as they related to principles and practices discussed in the course. Both graduate and undergraduate teacher education courses are now taught on a regular basis at professional development school sites.

School-Based Research

While the work of liaisons may be somewhat more labor intensive than traditional professorial duties, professional development schools offer many opportunities to conduct school-based research with practitioners on topics that will be used to answer questions and to solve problems in today's classrooms. Knowledge will be generated for the development of joint (university liaisons and preK-12 faculty) publications and national presentations as well as for immediate use in preK-12 classrooms. University liaisons and preK-12 teacher teams from the University of Memphis collaborative have made presentations on the work of the partnership and findings from research projects at conferences sponsored by the Tennessee Association for College Teacher Educators, Mid-South Educational Research Association, National Social Science Association, Association for Teacher Educators and the National Association for the Education of Young Children.

At one professional development school site, inquiries into and experimentation with cooperative learning strategies by a fourth-grade teacher-team resulted in positive changes in their classrooms. Some of the changes noted by the teacher-team were that students: (1) developed stronger social, problem solving, and verbal skills; (2) had more positive attitudes toward learning; (3) exhibited fewer discipline problems; (4) gained more confidence in themselves; (5) seemed glad to help each other learn; and (6) improved their grades in several areas (Morris et al. 1994).

What's more, school-based research studies have been conducted for the following purposes:

- To assess the needs of schools in selected areas (Morris, Taylor, Nunnery, Burr-McNeal, and Knight 1997).

- To evaluate pilot projects that have been undertaken (Lowther and Morrison 1997; Lowther, Morrison, and Abraham 1997; Morris, Branch, and Taylor 1995).

- To evaluate selected aspects of the professional development school partnership (Morris and Chance 1997; Morris, Taylor, Knight, and Mogge 1998; Morris, Chance, and Rakes 1996-99; Morris et al. 1994; Morris and Nunnery 1993).

Findings from these studies are being used to improve teaching and learning in professional development school classrooms, as well as the teacher education program at the university, and have generated data for publications and presentations at the state, regional, and national levels. For example, preK-12 teachers at one professional development school site expressed two concerns regarding the supervision of teachers in the first year of the program. They wanted cooperating teachers to be selected prior to the beginning of the term, and to receive more training in the supervision of teachers (Morris et al. 1994). As a result, both cooperating and student teachers at professional development school sites are informed of their placements during the prior semester.

Cooperating teachers receive data sheets on their prospective student teachers and are encouraged to call them. Student teachers are required to visit the classrooms of cooperating teachers prior to the beginning of their actual placement. The cooperating teachers also receive additional training in the supervision of student teachers. A mentoring program has been jointly developed by the local NEA affiliate, one of the school districts, and the university teacher education program. By the end of the second year, the faculty at this professional development school site indicated that their two concerns had been met. These findings and resulting changes have been reported in publications and professional presentations as noted earlier (Morris et al. 1994). By including preK-12 teachers and administrators as members of the research, writing, and presenting teams, the results aid in solving problems that had been identified by the preK-12 teachers and administrators.

Other Roles for University Professors

University professors who are not liaisons have become involved in professional development schools through a variety of partnership arrangements that include: conducting workshops based on needs identified in the school improvement plans; serving as consultants of grants, research, and classroom projects; and teaching on-site graduate courses requested by professional development schools classroom teachers to help implement their school improvement plans.

As the third year of the program began, new arrangements were planned to increase the presence of university faculty in professional development schools and to interest other faculty members in participating in the future. These included: (1) liaison teams of two university professors assigned to some professional development school sites (each one-quarter of their load) to share the partnership tasks; (2) university faculty from the arts and sciences serving in selected classrooms as content specialists; (3) university faculty invited to participate in periodic mini-conferences designed to meet needs-identified classroom teachers at PDSs, and (4) university faculty were invited to participate in the PDS year-end conferences and the national Symposium sponsored by the NEA Initiative on Teacher Educators. Both the preK-12 schools and the teacher education program at the university will profit from having university professors living in both worlds.

CONCLUSIONS

The role of university liaisons is critical to the successful implementation of professional development schools. The roles and responsibilities of university liaisons in professional development schools will vary, depending on whether the focus of the program involves inservice teachers, student teachers, the clinical experiences of prospective teachers enrolled in methods courses—or some combination of the three. At the University of Memphis, the focus is on inservice teachers and student teachers. Lessons learned regarding the roles, duties, and relationships of liaisons in our professional development school partnerships include the following:

1. *Time for reflection on practice.* As professional development schools evolve, it is essential that liaisons communicate on a regular basis, both formally and informally, about their experiences, accomplishments, failures, challenges, and concerns, while focusing on improving practice and relationships in their schools. Time for reflection allows the liaisons as a group to learn from one another and to model the collaboration process that is central to professional development school partnerships. Using this process, liaisons are able to share their experiences and to profit from those of liaisons at other professional development sites.

2. *Communication between monthly meetings.* Using electronic mail and other time-saving forms of communication may be the most efficient ways of exchanging instruction related to the

professional development school operation. This way, monthly or periodic team meetings of liaisons can be reserved for reflection on practice, related to issues that liaisons have agreed upon.

3. Orientation for liaisons. Orientation for liaisons should extend beyond information about supervising student teachers each semester. It should include information on: (1) the culture of the school and community, (2) the preK-12 schools' prior relationship with the the university, (3) activities that have been implemented in other professional development schools (both accomplishments and challenges), (4) roles and responsibilities of liaisons, and (5) roles and responsibilities of preK-12 administrators and classroom teachers. Because department chairs are responsible for personnel decisions—including assigning liaisons to professional development schools and evaluating liaisons for reappointment, tenure, and promotion—it is essential that they be active participants in the orientation sessions.

4. Stages of development of the university liaison's work. Year one for the university liaison in a professional development school may be primarily one of building rapport with preK-12 professionals. Classroom teachers who may suspect the motives of universities and their representatives need time to develop trust, collegiality, and a common purpose. While many goals may be accomplished during the first year, the liaison's work may proceed more effectively the second year, when preK-12 professionals, students, parents, and community people have begun to view the liaison as part of the school community. This process may differ from school to school in the same partnership.

5. Selection of professional development school university liaisons. Not every teacher educator can or should become a liaison in a professional development school, since special personal characteristics and qualifications are required to be effective. Liaisons should have a positive track record of teaching in preK-12 schools and as consultants or inservice workshop leaders in addition to working with teachers. They must be willing to make a long-term commitment to improve both the university's teacher education program and preK-12 teaching and learning. Effective liaisons view classroom teachers as equal partners in the teacher education process and are committed to playing a facilitative, rather than an "expert," role in improving schools.

6. Relationship between university liaison and principal. This relationship sets the tone for the liaison's work with classroom teachers and support staff. It it important that the principal and liaison clearly understand and respect one another's role in the partnership. While their approaches to teacher growth may be different, they should be complementary. As rapport and trust build, the liaison may become a peer, confidant, or mediator, and may be relied on to plan the school's inservice program. Principal and liaison roles may begin to blur as their relationship grows.

However, because the facilitative role of the liaison tends to empower teachers, there is potential for conflict. Jones (1993) reiterated this important lesson as it relates to the principal/liaison relationship. "There is real potential for mutual learning and support in this relationship. There is also potential for misunderstanding and conflict. It is the facilitator's [liaison's] responsibility to avoid power struggles (which she will probably lose, to no one's advantage)" (p. 139). The liaison should keep in mind that the work of the professional development school takes place on the principal's turf.

REFERENCES

Chance, L. 1992. *Professional Development Schools: Toward a New Relationship for K-12 Schools and Memphis State University.* Memphis, Tenn.: College of Education, Memphis State University.

Creaser, B. 1993. "Teachers as Observers of Play: Involving Teachers in Action Research." *Growing Teachers: Partnerships in Staff Development* (pp. 106-116). Edited by E. Jones. Washington, D.C.: National Association for the Education of Young Children.

Jones, E. 1993. "Growing teachers." *Growing Teachers: Partnerships in Staff Development* (pp. xii-xiii). Edited by E. Jones. Washington, D.C.: National Association for the Education of Young Children.

———. 1993. "Looking Back: What We've Learned About Partnerships." *Growing Teachers: Partnerships in Staff Development* (pp. 136-149). Edited by E. Jones. Washington, D.C.: National Association for the Education of Young Children.

Lowther, D. L. and G. R. Morrison. February 1997. "Project SMART: Changing One Classroom at a Time." Paper presented at the Association for Educational Communications and Technology National Conference, Albuquerque, N. Mex.

Lowther, D. L., G. R. Morrison, and K. Abraham. March 1997. "Professional Development for Successful Computer Integration." Paper presented at the 1997 Tennessee Educational Technology Conference, Nashville, Tenn.

Morris, V. G., E. Branch, and S. I. Taylor. 1995. *Improving the Literacy Skills of K-6 At-Risk Students Through Parental Involvement: Final Report on Student Success Program at Frayser Elementary School, 1994-95.* Memphis, Tenn.: College of Education, The University of Memphis. (ERIC Document Reproduction Service No. ED 386 448).

Morris, V. G. and L. Chance. 1997. "Customized Professional Development for In-service Teachers in a School-University Partnership." *British Journal of In-service Education*, 23 (3), 335-348.

Morris, V. G., L. Chance, and T. A. Rakes. 1996-97. "School Improvement Planning: A Critical Key in Urban School Reform." *National Forum of Teacher Education Journal*, 6 (2), 26-36.

Morris, V. G., S. I. Taylor, J. Knight, and K. Mogge. February 1998. "Mentor-Teaching As a Source of Professional Development in a School-University Partnership." Paper presented at the 79th Annual Meeting of the Association of Teacher Educators, Dallas, Tex.

Morris, V. G., S. I. Taylor, J. A. Nunnery, B. Burr-McNeal, and J. Knight. 1997. *Parent Efficacy, Teacher Efficacy, and Parent Involvement in Professional Development Schools: Research Report for Frayser Elementary School*. Memphis, Tenn.: College of Education, The University of Memphis. (ERIC Document Reproduction Service No. ED 399 219).

Morris, V. G., and J. A. Nunnery. 1993. *Teacher Empowerment in a Professional Development School Collaborative: Pilot Assessment* (Technical Report No. 931101). Memphis, Tenn.: Center for Research in Educational Policy, Memphis State University.

Morris, V. G., J. A. Nunnery, J. Scipio, J. Knight, M. Gopalakrishnan, and R. Rinehart. 1994. *A Case Study of Teacher Empowerment in a Professional Development School* (Technical Report No. 940101). Memphis, Tenn.: Center for Research in Educational Policy, Memphis State University.

Sid W. Richardson Foundation. 1992. *The Professional Development School: A Common Sense Approach to Improving Education*. Fort Worth, Tex.: A Report of the Sid W. Richardson Foundation Forum.

Chapter 5

ROLES AND RESPONSIBILITIES OF PARTICIPANTS IN PROFESSIONAL DEVELOPMENT SCHOOLS

by Robert C. Kleinsasser, Mary Jo Bird, Sr. Jean Marie Warne

The professional development school (PDS) concept has gained widespread attention in recent years, and various models and ways to implement them have been proposed (see Darling-Hammond 1994; Levine 1992; Wells 1993). In this chapter we examine the PDS model at the University of Memphis in terms of the changing roles and responsibilities of its participants. We relate how a variety of stakeholders have joined forces to improve our schools by encouraging collegiality between school and university through the training of preservice and inservice teachers.

PARTICIPANTS IN A PROFESSIONAL DEVELOPMENT SCHOOL

The various participants in our PDS experience include school faculty, administrators, preK-12 students, parents, community members, university faculty, and student teachers. With such a mix of people, it is difficult to keep communications free and open. Nonetheless, an *esprit de corps* requires nurturance, and all parties need to feel that their insights and ideas are an integral part of professional development and school improvement.

The Process

The process of forming a PDS is neither top-down nor bottom-up. Instead, it is a process that encourages interactions between school and university people who wish not only to prepare future teachers, but also to improve and extend educational knowledge.

Defining and implementing a PDS program requires all participants—not a select few—to begin discussion of the program's goals. Academic literature in the areas of school improvement and innovation needs to be reviewed and discussed. The university liaison is an important source of such information. Broad concepts of educational development must, of course, be adjusted to particular environments. In our particular situation the catalyst for educational knowledge development is the inservice education program.

Once the process begins, it becomes clear that both university and school personnel need to involve themselves in inservice development. While this requires extra time and effort on everyone's part, it also means that PDS members are involved in a continual learning and development process. Professional development schools are educational environments in action, and once given an opportunity to document and codify their actions, may be instrumental in providing educational knowledge in action to other professional development schools and colleagues around the state and country.

Cooperation, flexibility, and negotiation are key concepts in creating a successful PDS partnership. Needless to say, the element of time is also of crucial importance. Together, the partners must work to define (and perhaps to redefine) roles and responsibilities within their new professional development school. The following examples show how different participants have involved themselves in the PDS process.

Self-Directed Efforts

Some PDS sites have worked through a self-directed professional development sequence (Clark 1992) in order to give definition to their experience. In the beginning, faculty and university liaisons each wrote their own credos of teaching, reviewed their strengths, and outlined a five-year-plan. Such exercises served as catalysts for interaction and negotiation of meaning between school and university personnel. Their products eventually served as mission statements, future directions, and understandings about what the school and university had to offer each other.

In many cases, the new professional development schools built upon student teaching experiences, and this offered various avenues for defining what the PDS experience could be. The arrival of new student teachers each school semester requires some form of orientation meeting. Some schools created a general session where student teachers could be: (1) introduced to school protocols and philosophy, (2) given an overview of the student teaching program, and (3) taken on tours of the school grounds to meet staff members.

One PDS site developed a handbook specifically for its student teachers. Interestingly, some teachers had attempted to put together such a handbook numerous times in the past, without it ever really taking shape. With the help of the university liaison and suggestions from students and staff, a committee of teachers developed a handbook that continues to be revised each semester. Currently, this handbook contains over 20 pages of tips, guidelines, and other useful information.

Team teaching—which can involve the student teacher, the cooperating teacher, and the university liaison—offers classroom students the chance to participate in learning activities that one teacher may not readily attempt. It also affords an opportunity for preK-12 students to express their views about the classroom as they develop rapport with the university liaison. Team teaching can reinforce collaboration and collegiality among teachers, while also serving to show students that we are all learners and teachers at various points.

One PDS site tapped members of the community for funding and grant writing ideas. It also invited university faculty members to come and describe their methods to the whole school faculty. The university liaison at another school shared information about classroom observation. Faculty members welcomed the professor's insights and requested that she return to elaborate on how they could become better observers, not only of their student teachers, but of each other. This experience instigated further discussion about the observation process throughout the year.

These and numerous other examples demonstrate how collaboration and collegiality can help define various aspects of a professional development school program. We found that requests for help are rarely denied, and that the continual monitoring of forms of assistance by the university liaison, the school administration, and teachers helps to ensure that needs are actually being met. Obviously, the process of building a PDS must be fluid; directions for development are not dictated, but are planned, negotiated, and renegotiated among all participants as the program develops.

ROLES OF PARTICIPANTS

The roles of participants invariably are altered in any environment where negotiation, nurturance, and experimentation occur. The following discussion concentrates on the roles of preK-12 teachers and university liaisons in the PDS environment, while recognizing that other roles—those of students, parents, and school administrators—are also vital to the success of the program.

The Sharing of Evaluation

A unique and dynamic feature of our PDS is that both cooperating and support teachers (usually, teachers at the same grade level who do not have a student teacher) assume the traditional role of the university supervisor in evaluating student teachers. Due to their lengthy experience and daily use of lesson plans, these teachers are in a position to help student teachers in real life classrooms. They have firsthand knowledge of what the student teacher is doing, and can provide continual feedback, encouragement, and help. The cooperating teachers are not left alone with this new role. They attend professional development seminars and participate in an onsite university course in supervising student teachers. Additionally, they meet regularly with university liaisons who offer support in final evaluations.

Formal student teacher evaluations are the shared work of cooperating and support teachers, the school administrator, and the university liaison. It is important to emphasize how these participants take on new roles as they develop the evaluation process and guide student teachers in their professional growth. For instance, in implementing portfolio assessment at the elementary school level, they must decide on how to document evidence of growth in lesson plans, learning and teaching activities, and lesson presentations. Guiding this documentation are three questions: (1) What is the evidence? (2) Why does it serve as evidence? and (3) How does it demonstrate the student teacher's abilities? It is appropriate for the various participants to discuss the portfolio during intermittent conferences, so that the final portfolio can be used as a reference when the student teacher seeks employment, especially during job interviews.

The development of portfolio assessment in our professional development schools varies according to the particular needs, context, and faculty wishes at a PDS site. The traditional role of the university supervisor, who visited three or four times during a semester, has been replaced by the role of the classroom teacher as experienced professional. The new teacher-as-supervisor role works well in furthering the notions of collegiality and collaboration.

The Sharing of Teaching

The traditional role of the university supervisor has been transformed into that of university liaison, opening up new avenues for the university to extend and experiment with the professional development school process. No longer adhering to traditional supervision strategies, the university liaison's first job is to develop and nurture the PDS concept. Rather than coming in only to observe student teachers, liaisons visit their PDS sites on a regular basis. They provide assistance with staff development, and may also serve as team teachers, or even as substitute teachers for an hour or so. Their role extends to the conduct of meetings during the school day, especially once student teachers become more independent. These meetings can serve as opportunities for discussing concerns, ironing out problems, and sharing good experiences of the week.

The role of cooperating teachers similarly takes on different facets. In place of the traditional one-to-one relationship, a student teacher may be assigned to two or three cooperating teachers, each sharing the responsibility rather than assuming total charge. This allows a student teacher to teach the same subject at different levels, or to teach different subjects at the same grade level, as part of the internship experience. Even when a cooperating teacher assumes full responsibility for evaluation and mentoring, such responsibility is still shared with peers, helping to improve communication among faculty members. This type of arrangement also invites team teaching, which allows teachers to share teaching strategies with each other and to help student teachers in nonthreatening ways. With shared responsibility, classroom teachers no longer have to relinquish their classrooms and wonder what is occurring behind closed doors. The presence of more adults also encourages flexibility and provides much-needed release time for the entire teaching staff; and this, in turn, helps teachers better meet their goals and children's needs.

Meetings with a Purpose

Teachers in our professional development schools meet weekly with their university liaisons. These meeting are essential to the cohesiveness of the PDS process. Without time for direct communication, the aims and purpose of the program falter. Setting a weekly meeting time ensures that school faculty, administrators, and the university liaison come together to discuss the pressing issues of the day or week. Together, they brainstorm about how to improve the student teaching experience through the ways they teach and the ways they mentor. They share experiences—both positive and negative—concerning their relationships with school students, student teachers, and each other (teachers may even talk about their relationship with the liaison). All are welcome to offer items for the agenda and to discuss issues relating to the PDS concept.

Student teachers with each PDS site also meet weekly. These groups range in size from four to twenty members, depending upon the semester and the number of cooperating teachers. Their meetings serve not only as "group therapy" for the release of tension; they are also a time and place to discover what other student teachers are experiencing. This sharing can help student teachers better understand their professional development by discussing such issues as behavior management, lesson plans, portfolios, discipline problems, and other instructional and learning needs. At times, school faculty or administrators lead or participate in these meetings; at other times, guest speakers are invited. All in all, however, this time is reserved for student teachers to talk, share, complain, laugh, cry, and grow in understanding the profession they are entering.

The roles of all PDS participants have departed from tradition to embrace collaboration and collegiality. Mentoring student teachers is a joint effort by university and school personnel, and the traditional student teaching experience has been restructured and rejuvenated. Because all participants are more involved in the process, there is no limit to the valuable opportunities they encounter. A supportive partnership where student teachers can grow and learn under supervised care from both school and university is a growing reality in our professional development schools.

RESPONSIBILITIES OF PARTICIPANTS

As the PDS concept evolves, the responsibilities of its participants develop, alter, and progress. The university is no longer seen as the only place where teaching is taught, nor do university faculty have all the answers when it comes to instructional practice. PDS sites, too, offer on-site courses and provide insights into real teaching issues. Classroom teachers come to realize that university liaisons will "get their hands dirty" in the trenches if invited to do so. The community learns that universities and schools can create terrific learning environments when all work together for the benefit of students, the family, and society in general.

The Responsible University

It is the university's responsibility to nurture and support instruction in the schools. By offering a liaison, the university provides expertise and guidance with staff development. The liaison can serve as an extra staff member in the schools by team teaching or substitute teaching—giving teachers one or two extra hours to catch up on paper work, bulletin board development, or work on a unit of study. The university liaison can also offer a helping hand with discipline if the teacher wants to perform an activity requiring more student involvement and interaction. The liaison may even help correct homework assignments.

The responsibility of the university to share new knowledge and involve teachers in research also becomes paramount. The university can offer invaluable research opportunities to teachers seeking innovation, and can serve as a conduit for keeping schools abreast of workshops, seminars, and conferences. The university's grant writing specialist can be a wealth of information for supplementing school income. Moreover, its computer system allows for electronic mail, research, and field trips.

The university is responsible for respecting the needs of different educational environments, and it should attempt needs analysis to better understand what a particular school requires. The university should support both pre- and inservice staff development, and provide liaisons to create, implement, and nurture the PDS concept.

The Responsible School

The school's responsibility encompasses a broader mission when it becomes part of a PDS program. Not only does the school provide a student teaching site, it can offer inservice methods classes taught jointly by university and school personnel. By joining forces, the school and the university offer future teachers real life experiences followed up by discussions with experienced teachers, administrators, and college professors.

It is the school's responsibility to take a more hands-on approach to research. The school can open its doors to research, with teachers joining the research team to help develop relevant teacher education and guide classroom learning investigations. The ideas of school participants should be sought after and not ignored, and the school environment should encourage teachers to question, take risks, and try out innovative teaching and curricular ideas. Such a perspective may not be new, but it can be invigorating and offer great opportunities for growth.

The Responsible Community

The community's responsibility is to become more involved in the education of its students. Examples of how individuals within the community can extend a helping hand include: (1) volunteering for lunch duty; (2) aiding teachers with such task as correcting papers, making cut-outs for bulletin boards and art work, and accompanying field trips; and (3) providing materials for science and art projects. Businesses need to decide what they can offer the school and university partnership, not only in terms of monetary benefits, but also by providing opportunities for employees to volunteer in schools. They might volunteer to read to a child, guide a science experiment, or teach high school students how to write a resume (and what to do, so there is something to put on a resume). While the community's interest in the schools is represented by the school board, the PDS concept requires community members to involve themselves with more hands-on approaches. It aims to replace the "hit or miss" voluntary efforts of the past with a more coherent program.

In sum, the traditional model of school-community relations depended too heavily on certain teachers asking certain community members for help. The wealth of knowledge and assistance the community offers can no longer be ignored or used to benefit just a few classrooms or individuals. Schools must develop a plan for total community involvement, with the entire school reaping the numerous advantages such investment affords. No longer should parents ask what the school can do for them; they need to ask what they can do for their schools, the staff, and the children in them. Education is a community undertaking, and community members need to participate.

CONCLUSIONS

The PDS concept supports a collaborative approach to developing learning environments. We believe there is a need for all participants in the PDS process to restructure their roles and responsibilities. It is not an easy task, and it cannot be accomplished in a year or two. Instead, the process is one of constant change, with negotiation of our PDS partnership ever progressing. Rather than there being one right way to do things, we find there is a variety of ways to accomplish teaching and learning, and this is precisely what Kleinsasser (1993) suggests for a learning-enriched environment.

Teachers, students, the university liaison, and the community must all reflect on what learning is and how to go about it. Our goal is to effect change in order to produce literate citizens for the next generation. Teachers must work together to develop better learning environments, not only for students, but for themselves. Such an ethos nurtures creativity and development, enabling growth and rejuvenation in environments that have, at times, been stale, boring, and routine.

The restructuring of roles within our schools not only challenges tradition, but is at the heart of professional development schools. Roe and Kleinsasser (1993) suggest that ecological thinking, (considering the complexity of relations between teachers, students, and their total environment), cultural awareness, and communication among all participants are what will move our educational processes forward. Our experiences support this view.

REFERENCES

Clark, C. M. 1992. "Teachers as Designers in Self-Directed Professional Development." In *Understanding Teacher Development* (pp. 75-84). Edited by A. Hargreaves and M. G. Fullan. New York: Teachers College Press.

Darling-Hammond, L. (ed.). 1994. *Professional Development Schools: Schools for Developing a Profession.* New York: Teachers College Press.

Kleinsasser, R. C. 1993. "A Tale of Two Technical Cultures." *Teaching and Teacher Education: An International Journal of Research and Studies,* 9 (4): 373-383.

Levine, M. (ed.). 1992. *Professional Practice Schools: Linking Teacher Education and School Reform.* New York: Teachers College Press.

Roe, M. F. and R. C. Kleinsasser. 1993. "Delicate Balances: The Ecology, Culture and Communication of Reading Teachers." *Reading Research and Instruction,* 33 (2): 83-94.

Wells, G. (ed.). 1993. *Changing Schools from Within: Creating Communities of Inquiry.* Portsmouth, N.H.: Heinemann.

Chapter 6

A CONSENSUS-BUILDING MODEL FOR SCHOOL IMPROVEMENT

by Thomas Rakes, Lucindia Chance, Bonnie Cummings, Jane Trace, Nancy Harris, Sondra Chism

It is not surprising that during the early 1970s, when the most recent wave of school reform began, it was a school's adaptability—more than its efficiency—that caused others to view it as successful or effective. Organ (1971) makes this point in relation to changes in business, but the parallel in education is clear. In order to be effective, schools must embrace change, initiate ideas, and welcome planning as an ongoing process.

School planning is different from business planning in one important respect. Successful strategic planning in business is often executive or management driven, that is, top-down (Bradford and Duncan 2000; Carlson and Awkerman 1991). Developing school improvement plans, on the other hand, should be a site-based, staff driven, and cooperatively conceived process that includes a broad range of participants (Smylie, Bay and Tozer 1999). School planning requires strong administrative leadership, but it also calls for participation by faculty, students, and parents. This chapter describes a process for developing school improvement plans through a collaborative process. Unless representative parties are involved in the plan's creation, the final product will be viewed as another top-down effort.

KEY ELEMENTS OF A PLAN

School improvement plans need not be lengthy, but they should be specific enough to clearly reflect the tone, direction, values, uniqueness, and primary activities of a school. Key elements of the plan are a mission statement and six to eight primary goals, along with three to four measurable objectives for each goal. Simply stated, a usable school improvement plan should directly address these questions: "How do we go about planning for our school? What does this school believe is important? What areas of change are being addressed at this time?" A school improvement plan can provide the structure and focus necessary to communicate answers to these questions, as well as providing the guidance needed to deal with specific, school-based improvements. The development of a realistic school improvement plan begins with a conceived purpose or mission statement (Pascarella and Frohman 1989).

DETERMINING A MISSION STATEMENT

The importance of having a clearly defined mission statement cannot be overemphasized. Realistic, focused planning cannot begin without a specific statement of the organization's purpose or mission. It establishes the values, beliefs, and guidelines for the way in which the school conducts itself and determines its relationships with the individuals the school serves (Bradford and Duncan 2000; Carlson and Awkerman 1991). Appropriately formulated mission statements provide assurance that the improvement plans developed later will be focused and consistent with the mission of the school. A poorly conceived mission statement, on the other hand, may be so global and nonspecific that the uniqueness of its programs or its differences from other schools cannot be distinguished.

A mission statement should explain how the school operates and interacts with groups related to or affected by it. A statement should address the expectations of particular individuals representing student, faculty, and community interests. The following suggestions are offered as guidelines for creating a school mission statement. It should:

- be broader than a purpose or goal statement
- be brief (approximately 50-200 words in length)
- define the business of the school in general, flexible terms
- be a guide for the school's daily operations
- describe the population that the school serves
- include unique programs or characteristics of the school
- describe the beliefs and values of the school

Before beginning work on a school-specific mission statement, review any existing mission or philosophical statements issued by the board of education or central office. The school mission statement should be consistent with, and supportive of, such statements. Although some may suggest beginning with a needs assessment or issue analysis, we believe the mission of a school should be developed through a collaborative brainstorming type of experience with key faculty and administrators. A needs analysis should then be conducted as part of the actual planning process. Mission statements are not necessarily a reflection of what exists; rather, they delineate what is expected, what is important, and what is valued by those associated with a specific school.

Mission statements can be changed or refined as necessary, but they should not create a stumbling block that delays the planning process. Although it is typically best to include members outside the school in all of the following planning phases, the creation of a mission statement can bog down the whole planning process if too many people are involved initially. Teams of key faculty members and administrators should be responsible for developing drafts of a statement, which can then be reviewed for input from other teachers and groups of students in the school.

We also suggest that each school create its own mission statement before reviewing statements from other schools. After a draft has been created, sharing information with other schools may be helpful. This process may also help ensure that the special qualities of a school are addressed in its mission statement. Otherwise the team may create a look-alike statement that reads like several others.

DECIDING ON A PLANNING PROCESS

Having developed a mission statement, the next step is to decide on a specific process through which a usable school improvement plan can be made. If a school has recently completed a self-study or similar plan required by accreditation or a state agency, a school improvement plan can be created using existing data by adding specificity or updated needs to the plan. The steps are flexible and may be expanded or consolidated depending on your particular circumstances. Assuming that an existing plan or self-study is not being adapted or revised, the process shown in Figure 6.1 represents one method of putting a plan together. It may be necessary to adapt this multi-step process by adding or deleting a portion, depending upon the needs or situations in a particular school.

It is important to include representatives from community and parent interests as part of the initial writing process. External perspectives will serve to balance ideas and help develop support from a broader base of stakeholders. The second decision to be made involves the make-up of the initial planning teams. Do you want parents and teachers to participate in the development of goals and the needs survey? If so, everyone needs to be present at the first planning session involving the development of goals. One or more of the following steps can be accomplished during collaborative meetings with planning team members.

Steps in Planning

Major steps in developing an improvement plan:

1. Determine the composition of a planning team.
2. Schedule at least two initial two-hour planning sessions to develop 8-12 primary goals.
3. Gather information from others in two to three steps as a needs analysis (initial perceptions of goals).
4. Discuss inhibitors to accomplishing goals.
5. Prioritize goals.
6. Create measurable objectives, responsibilities, and timelines for objectives under each goal.
7. Implement the school improvement plan.
8. Review the success of the plan and revise for the future.

Appointing a Facilitator

After the creation of a mission statement and the selection of planning team members, a facilitator needs to be appointed. Should the principal, curriculum coordinator, lead teacher, university liaison, or someone else be responsible for working with the staff and committee groups to guide people through the process? The individual should be someone who is respected by the planning group members and who is openly receptive to ideas. We recommend that the university liaison be responsible for the initial sessions since the liaison is a part of the school, yet removed enough to be somewhat objective in viewing the organization. This may not be appropriate in all instances, but we have found such an arrangement to work well.

Alternatively, a college faculty member, a curriculum coordinator, or some other individual may have already established trust among staff members. Building-level administrators may not necessarily be the most appropriate persons to facilitate planning efforts. In some schools the principal or assistant principal is the best choice. However, in many instances, using school administrators as facilitators may be inappropriate if staff, students, and parents view such an appointment as an attempt to control or predetermine the outcome of the plan.

DETERMINING GOAL STATEMENTS

Gathering information from the planning committee is a critical part of a needs analysis. For this purpose, the use of several planning forms is recommended. Figure 6.2 includes a planning form for obtaining individual committee members' perceptions about what goals for the school should be. Participants should be given 15-20 minutes to complete the form without consultation or discussion with others. Each time groups are formed, regroup the members so that different people are continually being formed into groups of three, six, or more. For use in a particular school, it may be necessary to revise the categories or add lines for responses when using this, or other response forms, suggested for the planning process.

After individual lists of goals have been compiled, continue the process using Figure 6.3, Consensus Perceptions of Important Goals. This time have participants discuss their individual information in small groups of two or three people. This will encourage planning committee members to reach a consensus, and to consolidate their goals into a single list. After the small group lists are generated, reconvene members into new, medium-size groups of six or eight people, and use Figure 6.4 to continue the process.

The purpose of the series of three regrouping, re-organizing exercises involving goal setting is to ensure that broad and thorough consideration is given to perceived goals for several constituencies. Such a procedure not only enables groups of individuals to work toward common areas of need, but it also provides people with an opportunity to discuss what they think is important for different groups in the school. The process we are recommending requires more front-end time than simply convening a small group, having them survey others, and then writing a plan and circulating it for review. This broad involvement is critical in avoiding the perception that it is simply a top-down effort.

DETERMINING INHIBITING FACTORS

With the information created by the discussion of goals, it is appropriate to take time to consider factors, conditions, and situations that planning members perceive to be keeping the school from meeting its goals. Figure 6.5 includes a suggested format for discussing inhibiting factors. Once possible impeding factors are discussed, it will be time to revisit the middle group goal statements, and regroup as two or three large groups to create one prioritized list of goals. It is not unusual for groups to need 30-60 minutes to consider what seems to be holding them back. It may be necessary to dedicate one to two goals to problems such as school environment or safety needs.

School improvement plans ought to focus on what is possible, but they should also include elements of what should be, even to the point of being somewhat idealistic in sections. For example, one professional development school included in its plan a single goal involving the generation of grants for external funding to meet technology-related needs. Grant writing seminars were held, and teams began to write grants, even though the school had no previous track record involving major grant writing. Faculty members knew how difficult it was to secure external funding for equipment purchases. Yet, within twelve months, the school had secured several small grants of a few hundred dollars each, and one grant totaling just under $200,000 to equip eight classrooms with computers.

During its first year as a professional development school, another school was in the process of changing from a junior high school to a middle school. In this instance, the school improvement plan was heavily focused on issues and topics associated with this major organizational change. Both of these successful efforts emerged as a direct result of goal setting and objectives generated as part of the collaborative process used to develop a school improvement plan. All goals in the plans were not met, but the successes were so great that teachers were eager to review and revise the plans for the next year.

PRIORITIZING MAJOR GOALS

Use the form provided in Figure 6.6 to assist planning members in determining a prioritized list of goals. At this point, group members have spent two or three sessions working through individual, small, and medium group discussions before getting to the large group setting. Be sure to allow sufficient time for the various stages of discussion. It is not unusual for planning sessions involving prioritizing goals to last 60-90 minutes.

DEVELOPING AN ACTION PLAN

The final stage in developing a school improvement plan involves adding one to three specific objectives with supporting information for each major goal statement. Figure 6.7 represents a suggested format for creating usable objectives with accompanying information. All categories included in the form for creating objectives may not be appropriate for use in all schools. Different categories may also need to be used in addition to, or in place of, those used in Figure 6.7.

OBSTACLES TO OVERCOME

The following list represents several considerations that may be of value to those who facilitate or become actively involved in the planning process for developing a school improvement plan. The information has been adapted from Sterner (1979), who described pitfalls in planning for managers in a corporate setting.

Obstacles in Getting Started

1. Failing to select a facilitator who is capable of encouraging communications and staying on task.
2. Assuming that meaningful change can be fostered without careful and collaborative deliberations among a wide range of interested people.
3. Delaying the creation of a school improvement plan because of the current level of success.
4. Assuming that meaningful changes can be made without having a usable plan and an ongoing process for monitoring improvements.

Obstacles Related To Misunderstanding the Nature of Planning a School Improvement Plan

   5. Forgetting that planning is a political, social, and organizational process.
   6. Assuming that the master plan for the school district is sufficient for every school.
   7. Assuming that planning does not need to include everyone involved in the school.
   8. Assuming that planning is easy.
   9. Assuming that plans cannot be developed and actually used.

Obstacles in Developing a School Improvement Plan

   10. Administrators who are so engrossed in existing situations that they spend little time participating in the planning process.
   11. Failing to include both short (one year or less) and long range goals in the plan.
   12. Failing to take front-end time to include many people in the process
   13. Assuming that equal weight should be given to all goals and objectives.
   14. Insisting on so much structure that planning cannot tolerate creative, visionary ideas.
   15. Failing to write measurable objectives.
   16. Assuming that most old methods or ideas need changing.

Obstacles in Implementing a School Improvement Plan

   17. Forgetting that the purpose of a school improvement plan is to focus on specific school-based needs and to determine alternative ways for meeting these needs.
   18. Assuming that completed plans are finished products and must be followed to the letter.
   19. Ignoring plans in order to maintain the status quo.
   20. Failing to use plans as one measure of school effectiveness.
   21. Failing to recognize and reward those individuals who actively participate and make positive contributions to the planning and change process.

CONCLUSIONS

A completed school improvement plan should contain a mission statement along with a list of goals and objectives, and a closing page describing a plan for revising the plan. At the beginning and the end of each school year, the plan should be studied and a determination made as to which goals and objectives were met, and which need to be extended, deleted, or revised. We recommend that prior to making these decisions, the person(s) responsible for individual items should be contacted. Whenever possible, it is wise to obtain a written explanation from the responsible person(s) as to the status of an objective. It is also important to be sure that responsible persons are reminded of the duties associated with the school improvement plan at the beginning of each year, and at least in December or January of the school year. When objectives are met, it is important to capitalize on success by publicly recognizing those responsible and drawing attention to the strategies they used to meet the objective.

The need for organized planning in professional development schools is critical. The previously described process may not be entirely appropriate for all situations. It may be necessary to add or delete steps and revise the sample forms included in this discussion. Regardless of these adaptations, the school improvement plan should serve as the guiding force for generating change within the school. It is paramount that we realize that the most successful change comes from collaborative planning.

Figure 6.1

Outline for a Consensus-Building Model For Developing School Improvement Plan

The following list reflects the recommended steps to be used in developing a school improvement plan.

1. Develop a mission statement for the school.

2. Develop individual perceptions of important goals. (Figure 6.2)

3. Develop small group perceptions of important goals. (Figure 6.3)

4. Develop medium group perceptions of important goals. (Figure 6.4)

5. Consider inhibiting factors. (Figure 6.5)

6. Develop large group (full faculty) prioritized listing of perceived goals. (Figure 6.6)

7. Develop action plans. (Figure 6.7)

Figure 6.2

Individual Perceptions of Important Goals

DIRECTIONS: Work alone and in the space provided write the major goals for this school as you believe they are most commonly perceived by:

1. Students:

2. Faculty:

3. School Administration:

4. Parents/Community:

5. Support Staff:

Figure 6.3

Small Group Perceptions of Important Goals

DIRECTIONS: Work in groups of 2-3 people, and in the space provided write the major goals for this school as your group believes they are most commonly perceived by:

1. Students:

2. Faculty:

3. School Administration:

4. Parents/Community:

5. Support Staff:

Figure 6.4

Medium Group Perceptions of Important Goals

DIRECTIONS: Work in groups of 6-8 people, and in the space provided consolidate previous lists into one list of major goals for this school as your group believes they are most commonly perceived by:

1. Students:

2. Faculty:

3. School Administration:

4. Parents/Community:

5. Support Staff:

Figure 6.5

Inhibiting Factors

DIRECTIONS: Working in new groups of 4-6 people, brainstorm to determine what factors or conditions are causing the school to fail to meet its existing goals. Use the space below to list the factors and then share your information with the other groups.

1.

2.

3.

4.

5.

6.

7.

8.

9.

Figure 6.6

Large Group Prioritized Listing of Perceived Goals

DIRECTIONS: Using your medium group listing of goal statements, discuss and attempt to gain consensus on 1-2 goals for each segment of your interested parties. If the group is too large, form groups of 5-6 people for each of the majors sections (e.g., students, faculty, staff, community. . .) Be specific in stating measurable outcomes. If the space provided is not sufficient, write on the back of this sheet. Be sure to take time to share your information with all groups after you have finished.

For Students:

1.

2.

3.

For Faculty:

1.

2.

3.

For Parents/Community:

1.

2.

3.

For School Administration:

1.

2.

3.

For Support Staff:

1.

2.

3.

For Others:

1.

2.

3.

Figure 6.7

Action Plans

DIRECTIONS: Working in groups of 3-4 people, select one or more goals and create 1-2 specific and measurable objectives including the additional information requested for each objective. These goals with objectives will be used as the functional portion of the school improvement plan (along with the mission statement).

For Students:

Goal 1.
Objective:

Benchmark/Resources:

Completion Date:
Person Responsible:

Goal 2.
Objective:

Benchmark/Resources:

Completion Date:
Person Responsible:

For Teachers:

Goal 1.
Objective:

Benchmark/Resources:

Completion Date:
Person Responsible:

Goal 2.
Objective:

Benchmark/Resources:

Completion Date:
Person Responsible:

For Parents/Community:

Goal 1.
Objective:

Benchmark/Resources:

Completion Date:
Person Responsible:

Goal 2.
Objective:

Benchmark/Resources:

Completion Date:
Person Responsible:

For Support Staff:

Goal 1.
Objective:

Benchmark/Resources:

Completion Date:
Person Responsible:

Goal 2.
Objective:

Benchmark/Resources:

Completion Date:
Person Responsible:

For School Administration:

Goal 1.
Objective:

Benchmark/Resources:

Completion Date:
Person Responsible:

Goal 2.
Objective:

Benchmark/Resources:

Completion Date:
Person Responsible:

REFERENCES

Bradford, R. W. and J. P. Duncan. 2000. *Simplified Strategic Planning: A No-Nonsense Guide for Busy People Who Want Fast Results.* Worcester, Mass.: Chandler House Press.

Carlson, R. V. and G. Awkerman (eds.). 1991. *Educational Planning: Concepts, Strategies, and Practices.* White Plains, N.Y.: Longman.

Organ, D.W. 1971. "Linking Pins Between Organizations and Environment." *Business Horizons*, 14(6): pp.73-80.

Pascarella, P. and M.A. Frohman. 1989. *The Purpose-Driven Organization: Unleashing the Power of Direction and Commitment.* San Francisco: Jossey-Bass.

Steiner, G. A. 1979. *Strategic Planning: What Every Manager Must Know.* New York: The Free Press.

Chapter 7

TEACHER EMPOWERMENT: HOW DOES IT EMERGE?

by Vivian Gunn Morris, John Nunnery,
   Satomi Izumi Taylor, Janie Knight, Pat Brooks

If schools are to make meaningful change, teachers must have significant input regarding what happens in them. Professional development schools provide a framework for this simple, but powerful, observation. In a professional development school, "teachers are viewed as knowledgeable and committed workers who seek a greater voice in decisions affecting their work and who, in return, are willing to accept responsibility for these decisions" (Nystrand 1991, p. 3).

The professional development school (PDS) movement, rooted in the traditions of laboratory, campus, and portal schools (Stallings and Kowalski 1992), has in recent years demonstrated its strong commitment to increasing the degree to which teachers are empowered to make educational decisions that can bring about change in our schools. Laboratory schools have a long history in serving as university campus schools, while portal schools—which serve as "a point of entry for promising new curricula and practices"—are more recent in their origin (Chambers and Olmstead 1971).

EMPOWERING TEACHERS

What exactly is empowerment? Wellins, Byham, and Wilson (1991) have explicated the concept of empowerment in a business context:

> Power means "control, authority, dominion." The prefix em- means "to put on to" or "to cover with." Empowering, then, is passing on authority and responsibility (p. 22).

Wellins et al. (1991) further suggest specific connotations of empowerment:

> As we refer to it here, empowerment occurs when power goes to employees who then experience a sense of ownership and control over their jobs. . . . Empowered individuals know that their jobs belong to them. Given a say in how things are done, employees feel more responsible. When they feel responsible, they show more initiative in their work, get more done, and enjoy the work more (p. 22).

While the concepts of teacher empowerment and employee empowerment probably share the same denotation, empowerment of teachers appears to have connotations other than, or in addition to, a sense of control and increased responsibility. These connotations reflect the contextual specificity of the empowerment concept when applied to the teaching profession.

Various authors have suggested purposes, means, or dimensions of teacher empowerment that connote enrichment of the empowerment concept. For example, Romanish (1991) argues that the primary purpose of teacher empowerment is to improve teaching and learning experiences in the classroom. Romanish's model of an empowered teacher incorporates the teacher's belief in his or her ability to act—an ability tied to capable action. According to this model, not only do empowered teachers have decision-making power in the classrooms, but they also have authority to significantly influence decisions related to education at the school or system level. Therefore, Romanish's model includes a dimension of professionalism which reflects a belief that empowered teachers participate in control of the profession and the settings in which educators function. Control of the profession may include determining who is inducted into the profession, as well as who has responsibility for teacher education. Yonemura (1987) identifies three paths to the empowerment of teachers: (1) creating curricula, (2) fostering peer relationships, and (3) facilitating study that promotes shifts in perspectives about children. Team membership and the sharing of knowledge with peers are dimensions of empowerment noted by Fay (1992). Maeroff (1988) suggests that teachers must achieve professional status, knowledge, and access to decision making to be empowered.

Five Dimensions of Empowerment

A conceptualization of teacher empowerment that encompasses each of these authors' views would include dimensions related to: (1) collegiality, (2) influence over entrance to the profession—including mentoring student teachers, (3) decision-making power, (4) professional knowledge, and (5) teaching self-efficacy. These five dimensions of teacher empowerment are addressed within this chapter. The dimensions are discussed within the context of the four major program components that make up the PDS model at the University of Memphis (see Figure 7.1). These four components—supervision of practice teachers, school improvement planning, clinical professor training, and applied research and inquiry—are examined in light of the following questions:

1. To which dimensions of teacher empowerment does this component relate?

2. What conditions or prerequisites are necessary in order to implement this component in a manner that promotes teacher empowerment?

3. How do participant experiences and research findings about the implementation of the PDS model at the University of Memphis inform our understanding of the relationships between specific program components and the emergence of teacher empowerment?

Data for this chapter were collected from 114 teachers who completed a Teacher Empowerment Survey. These teachers were employed in five elementary schools that are partners in our PDS collaborative. At one of the five schools, Friar Tuck, additional qualitative methods were used to collect data related to the four major components of the PDS program. Methods used included participation observation, in-depth interviews, focus groups, and examination of archival materials.

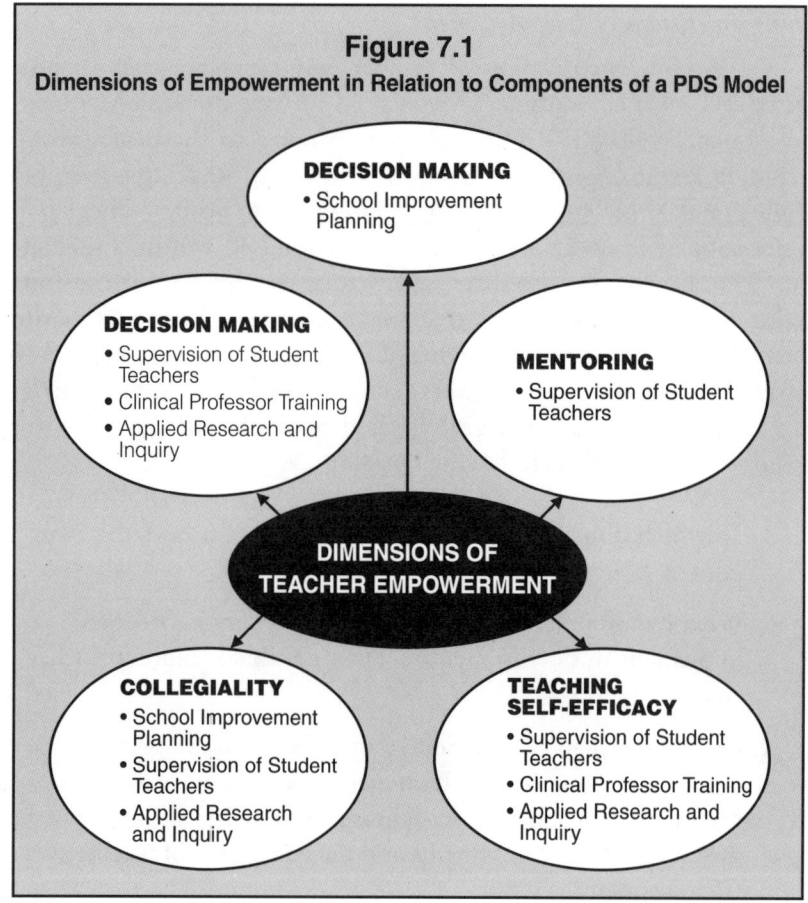

Figure 7.1
Dimensions of Empowerment in Relation to Components of a PDS Model

SUPERVISION OF STUDENT TEACHERS

For all too long, the universities and the preK-12 schools maintained the status quo: The universities were supposed to prepare students to become teachers, and the schools were supposed to prepare students to become productive citizens.

Because of this rigid separation of roles, the roles of the key participants in teacher education—the student teacher, the cooperating teacher, and the university liaison, formerly called the "university representative" or "university supervisor"—were also separate. Customarily, the university liaison's primary role was to make several visits to observe the student teacher in the cooperating teacher's classroom. The university liaison would then organize a conference with the student teacher and the cooperating teacher. The cooperating teacher's role was merely a supporting one: to give input regarding the student teacher's performance as needed. However, with the emergence of professional development schools, these roles are changing. (See Chapter 5.)

Teachers Are Leaders

Our PDS model acknowledges that the person most qualified to take the lead in preparing the student teacher may not be the university liaison, but rather the cooperating teacher.

Why is this so? Because no matter how much involvement the university liaison has with the school, the cooperating teacher undoubtedly has a greater degree of involvement with the student teacher. The cooperating teacher is the one who, day after day, watches the student teacher at work and provides the student teacher with constant and appropriate informal feedback. The cooperating teacher is the one who watches some lessons fail, others succeed, and still others fall somewhere in between the two extremes. Weeks of this give-and-take transpire prior to the first progress report evaluation attended by the university liaison.

The cooperating teacher may also possess characteristics well suited to the supervisory role. For example, the cooperating teacher may excel in roles such as mentoring, coaching the student teacher in skill development, serving as a professional role model, possessing confidence in professional knowledge, having an awareness of individual styles of teaching, and being willing to work with other teachers to improve schoolwide teaching and learning (Morris et al. 1994).

The Teacher Empowerment Survey conducted by the PDS program at the University of Memphis elicited information about these characteristics, and provides documentation of their existence among teachers selected for participation in PDS sites. Items included on the survey's mentoring self-efficacy scale were related to the supervision of student teaching component. In their responses, 74 percent of Friar Tuck teachers and 79 percent of the comparison teachers indicated that they became more sensitive to the problems and stress experienced by student teachers as a result of their participation in the PDS program. (See Table 7.1 for more details.)

Will Change Occur?

By taking the lead in supervising and evaluating student teachers, the cooperating teacher can become empowered to share in deciding who enters the teaching profession. However, in considering a PDS model that encourages the cooperating teacher to take on the roles of mentor and supervisor, we have two reservations: Will the cooperating teacher really accept this change in perspective? And will the university liaison be able to help bring about this change in perspective?

The answer to the first question is Yes. Each school that has been selected as one of our PDS sites can attest to the fact that, indeed, the role of the cooperating teacher has changed. University liaisons have reported that teachers have gained confidence and satisfaction in taking the lead in the progress report conferences. Cooperating teachers' leadership during conferences has proven to be a significant step in the PDS process and one that clearly demonstrates the teachers' empowerment.

To address the second question, we need to look at the clinical professor training component of our PDS model. During the 51 hours of clinical professor training, cooperating teachers learn to enhance their skills as educators. In each site, the training is designed to mesh with the needs identified in the school's improvement plan. Topics chosen in several of our PDS sites include: supervision, mentoring, and evaluation of student teachers; improving students' reading scores; classroom management; and parental involvement. In some cases, teachers reported that they had not fully understood that 51 hours of training were required. Though these teachers may have felt that the time requirement for training was too great, most teachers appeared appreciative of the opportunity to increase their professional knowledge in needed areas. Upon completion of the clinical professor training, the teachers are designated as adjuncts of choice in the University's College of Education. This designation has done much for the teachers' self-esteem as well as their esteem by peers.

Each PDS assumes a life of its own, making a commitment to collaboration and becoming a structure within which change can occur. However, when changes in traditional roles and responsibilities are made, individuals and organizations often experience growing pains. Supervisory experiences in our PDS sites have been filled with both positive and negative experiences. While teachers often praise the leadership role they are offered, they are sometimes resistant to the extra training—for example, training in reflective mentoring—required to fulfill their leadership role.

Although the cooperating teacher's supervisory role requires much change, it is the cornerstone of the PDS model that proposes to redesign the student teaching and inservice experiences of all key participants—the student teacher, the cooperating teacher, and the university liaison.

SCHOOL IMPROVEMENT PLANNING

School improvement planning is linked to the emergence and enhancement of teacher empowerment in the areas of decision making, collegiality, and teaching self-efficacy. However, before collegiality and teaching self-efficacy can be significantly enhanced, teachers must be confident of their power to make decisions. They must believe that their decisions matter and will be honored.

Although teachers constantly make on-the-spot decisions in the classroom, they may have experienced little decision-making power outside the classroom. Real empowerment related to decision making is more than participation in teacher committees that advise the principal; in real empowerment, teachers make decisions affecting not only their own classrooms and schools, but also their districts and state. Some decision-making opportunities at the school level that can contribute to school improvement planning and enhance teacher empowerment are: (1) developing alternative assessment programs, (2) selecting textbooks and curriculum approaches that are developmentally appropriate, and (3) sharing in personnel and budget decisions (Foster 1992). These are areas in which decisions have historically been made by administrators at the school, district, or state level.

Effective school improvement planning requires that teachers and administrators work with and influence their peers to improve teaching and learning. If an open, trusting, and accepting school climate is created by the principal, teachers are more willing to believe that their opinions will be heard and valued by both administrators and peers. This spirit of trust allows collegiality to emerge or to be enhanced.

The empowerment dimensions of decision making and collegiality are inherently connected to the dimension of teaching self-efficacy. The belief by teachers that their decisions matter and can influence administrators and peers creates the opportunity for their teaching self-efficacy to emerge or to be enhanced. Using school improvement planning, teachers begin to feel an increased sense of status, self-esteem, and professionalism.

In our PDS model, each school faculty was required to develop a school improvement plan organized around an understanding of the goals of five constituencies: students, faculty, school administrators, central office administrators, and parents and communities. In each site, faculty and staff worked together in setting priorities for training and implementation. Each site's school improvement plan was the driving force for inservice on-site workshops that were implemented during the year.

Included in the action plans at one of the PDS sites, Friar Tuck Elementary, were literature reviews in selected areas, grant writing activities, visits to classrooms in other schools, and participation and facilitation by preK-12 teachers at workshops. Under the plan, each grade level committee developed a written school improvement report to be presented at an end-of-year meeting; suggested topics for the reports were workshop sessions, new classroom strategies, and areas of interests for future school improvement plans. Specifically, the Friar Tuck school improvement plan called for focus on developmentally appropriate practice, nongraded primary, whole language learning, cooperative learning, building self-esteem, and planning field trips. Inservice workshops were conducted for the Friar Tuck faculty on these topics with additional sessions devoted to supervising, evaluating and mentoring student teachers.

Measuring Teachers' Perceptions

According to information reported in the Teacher Empowerment Survey, less than half of the teachers at Friar Tuck (47 percent) and at other selected PDS sites (46 percent) had increased their participation in schoolwide decision making as a result of participation in the PDS program. This perception may be related to at least two factors. First, while school faculties voted to participate in the PDS program, many decisions regarding how the program would be implemented during the pilot year were made without input from the teachers. This includes the number of hours for clinical professor training and the model used for the school improvement planning process. Teachers probably did not begin to feel the impact of these decisions until the implementation phase of the program, the phase in which the Teacher Empowerment Survey was conducted. Secondly, because of guidelines mandated by the state and the local school board, teachers believed that their hands were often tied in making desired curriculum changes mentioned in school improvement planning discussions.

Faculty members at Friar Tuck were actively involved in developing the school improvement plan and selected topics for the inservice workshops. The responses found below are typical of teachers' remarks relative to their input in decision making:

> I think the input has been during the inservice meetings when ... [the university liaison] would ask what we needed and she would always take whatever we'd done that day, compile it, and bring it back so we could work on it. We were constantly given opportunity to provide input into how that plan progressed during the year.

> We did have input into the school improvement plan, but we were not part of the decision making on any other part of it, as far as whether we would actually be in it or not, or we knew nothing about the hours or years involved. We had no part in the decision making of any of that. I think had we had some decision making in that, it would have been less stressful, there would have been a lot more cooperation from the very beginning, and I think there would have been a sense of overall accomplishment at the end. Any time you're part of a decision-making group, you get a sense of owning whatever you're doing. We had no ownership at all, until we literally began to be involved with this school improvement plan. And it took a while, I think, because we were not in on all of it from the beginning. (Morris et al. 1994, pp. 25-26)

The experiences of teachers at Friar Tuck Elementary indicate that the school improvement process did foster enhanced collegiality. More than 69 percent of Friar Tuck teachers reported enhanced empowerment along each of the four items included in the collegiality dimension. Sixty-nine percent of Friar Tuck teachers, versus 62 percent of teachers at other selected PDS sites, felt that as a result of their involvement in the PDS program, they talked more with other teachers, while 72 percent of teachers in both groups indicated they were more willing to assist other teachers who were experiencing problems. Seventy-five percent of Friar Tuck teachers, versus 67 percent of comparison teachers, indicated that they participated in a greater amount of cooperative planning with other teachers. Additionally, 78 percent at Friar Tuck, versus 74 percent of comparison teachers, felt they were more willing to share and work with peers to improve teaching and learning at their schools. (See Table 7.2.)

Through the process of developing a comprehensive program for their school, teachers at Friar Tuck had many opportunities to share their opinions and ideas regarding goals, objectives, and activities required to make their school a learning community for children, teachers, parents, and administrators. Teachers shared their ideas in written and oral forms with their peers at their specific grade level, across grade levels, and with support teachers and administrators.

Enhanced empowerment along the teaching self-efficacy dimension also appears to have been influenced by the school improvement planning process. More than 70 percent of Friar Tuck teachers reported enhanced empowerment on three of the six items of this particular dimension. Seventy-nine percent of Friar Tuck teachers, versus 78 percent of comparison teachers, indicated they were more aware of the influence they could have in improving teaching and learning, and 72 percent, versus 68 percent of comparison teachers, felt an increased sense of professionalism. Eighty-one percent of Friar Tuck teachers, versus 73 percent of comparison teachers, indicated they had increased self-confidence as professional role models. (See Table 7.3.)

When interviewed, teachers at Friar Tuck reported that the major benefits of the school improvement planning process were knowledge gained about different teaching strategies (professional knowledge dimension) and improved communication among faculty across grade levels (collegiality). The following comments of teachers emphasize the benefits noted:

> Just to do a school improvement plan would make you have to communicate. If you hadn't been communicating before, you would communicate. It will open the door, even if it starts out very slowly.

Has the school improvement plan itself helped me to integrate better into the school system? It has made me more aware of all the faculty members and the community. It lets me know what they are doing in the classroom, what's happening in the other classrooms. I know that next door cooperative learning is taking place, and I know what is happening with the computer system, because everybody keeps in contact and lets me know what skills my students need to be working on. So I think it has helped. By being a new teacher, it has been a little friendlier and forces people not to hide all of the good ideas they have.

As we were discussing and working on the school improvement plan, we might talk about whole language, for example, or cooperative learning, and we might discuss how someone had tried that on a particular grade level and what did work and what didn't work. And when you go back and try it with your grade level, certain parts might work with one of those age groups but not with another. So it was just different things that came out in the work we did in inservice. I think there was more consensus within the faculty as to what was needed from grade level to grade level after that. (Morris et al. 1994, p. 18)

EMPOWERMENT THROUGH TRAINING

The clinical professor training component is linked to the emergence and enhancement of empowerment in the areas of professional knowledge and teaching self-efficacy. When teachers feel that they have improved in subject matter and pedagogical skills, they feel more empowered along both the professional knowledge dimension and the teaching self-efficacy dimension. Teachers display confidence that they are capable professionals, able to make sound decisions based on their knowledge. The clinical professor training therefore enhances teachers' sense of status, self-esteem, and professionalism.

In our PDS model, teachers are engaged in ongoing professional development that responds to the priorities listed in the faculty's school improvement plan. The list of topics cited within the plan is used to select a pool of professionals capable of conducting workshops on these topics. Professionals are expected to provide the training at the school site during clinical professor training sessions.

At all of our PDS sites, clinical professor training was delivered on school sites by professionals from the College of Education. Many topics were covered, including stages of the student teacher, evaluation of student teachers, clinical supervision, reflective mentoring, classroom management, grant writing, and school improvement planning. Other topics that emerged as time passed were: parental involvement, reading in the elementary school, special needs children, cooperative learning, whole language, test anxiety of students, effective schools for children at risk, and developmentally appropriate practices.

Teachers in the PDS sites felt that the clinical professor training component of the program enhanced empowerment along the teaching self-efficacy dimension. They felt that knowledge gained about different teaching strategies, as well as communication among faculty across grade levels, helped teachers to gain more confidence in what they were doing and in their ability to do it well. Enhanced empowerment along the teaching self-efficacy dimension was measured by administering the professional knowledge and teaching self-efficacy scales of the Teacher Empowerment Survey. Additional information was gathered from individual interviews, questionnaires, and focus group discussions. In the teaching self-efficacy dimension, 78 percent to 79 percent of all the teachers indicated that after the clinical professor training and implementation of the strategies learned, they were more aware of the influence they could have in improving teaching and learning. (See Table 7.3.) Seventy-three to 81 percent of the teachers indicated that they also had increased self-confidence as professional role models.

Table 7.4 shows that 75 percent of the teachers felt enhanced empowerment in the area of awareness of individual styles of teaching. There was, however, a wide range of responses among schools concerning teachers' confidence in their ability to help or teach at-risk students. Teachers at one school had a large population of at-risk students. Therefore, they had received more clinical professor training on at-risk topics and reported stronger confidence in their ability to deal with at-risk children.

Teachers found some clinical professor training sessions more beneficial than others. Teachers were especially pleased when they had input on the selection of topics for workshop sessions, and when university liaisons were able to quickly secure resource people to address requested topics. By working with the university, teachers felt that more resources were available to meet their needs than ever before. They were also pleased to have workshop sessions at their school site rather than across the city and to have small group sessions rather than systemwide inservice meetings featuring a large number of professionals.

However, the amount of time spent in clinical professor training emerged as a major concern of teachers. Many reported that two hours after school on a weekly basis made for a long, tiring day and, often, an ineffective session. Some of the alternatives suggested by the teachers were: (1) to schedule the training during support periods as well as after school, (2) to offer concentrated weekend courses (Friday evening through Saturday), (3) to allow voluntary faculty participation, and (4) to register teachers in advance to assure that resources would be available for all in attendance.

APPLIED RESEARCH AND INQUIRY

The applied research and inquiry component of a PDS program is linked to teacher empowerment along the dimensions of professional knowledge, collegiality, and teaching self-efficacy. As classroom teachers become reflective practitioners and action-researchers, they are able to research those topics that are related to their own needs. Facilitated by technical training and support provided by the university, they become not only consumers of knowledge but also creators of knowledge. They have many opportunities to share their new knowledge with colleagues at the school, district, state, and national levels. This role of researcher, which is a new one for many teachers, also has the potential to enhance collegiality and teaching self-efficacy.

Fostering Research by Teachers

In our PDS model, teachers' interest in research was fostered in a variety of ways. Workshop presenters placed emphasis on relevant research data to support their recommendations. The director of development for the College of Education conducted workshops on grant writing and offered continuing technical support as teachers' grant writing got underway. For example, several of the faculty teams at Friar Tuck Elementary wrote grants and gave input to grants written by the university liaison.

At Friar Tuck Elementary, each grade level committee selected an area from the school improvement plan for implementation during the second semester of the school year. Teachers selected activities in the following areas: developmentally appropriate practice, nongraded primary, field trips, whole language, cooperative learning, and building self-esteem. The committees' school improvement reports indicated that during the academic year they had completed preliminary literature searches, developed grant proposals, attended conferences, and visited classrooms in other schools in the city. When adequate literature searches were not available in their own professional libraries, the University liaison brought resources from the University and conducted ERIC searches to provide the needed references.

More than 70 percent of Friar Tuck teachers reported enhanced empowerment along two of the six items included in the professional knowledge dimension, probably in part as a result of their participation in grant writing activities. (See Table 7.4.) Seventy-five percent of teachers in the PDS sites indicated that they were more aware of individual styles of teaching. Seventy-four percent of Friar Tuck teachers, versus 51 percent of teachers at the other PDS sites, felt increased confidence in their ability to help or teach students who were at risk for school failure.

Cooperative Learning at Friar Tuck

While no formal research projects were conducted during Friar Tuck's first year of implementing the program, teachers presented their accomplishments in both written and oral presentations at the final inservice meeting for the year. One grade level committee noted the following changes as a result of implementing cooperative learning groups in that grade's classrooms:

1. More students were actively involved in the learning process.
2. Students enjoyed learning from each other.
3. Students improved their social skills.
4. Students showed stronger problem solving skills.
5. Student learned more about each other.
6. Students' interests increased in many subject areas.
7. Students displayed stronger verbal skills.
8. There was an improved classroom environment.
9. Discipline problems decreased.
10. Grades improved in many areas.
11. Students had more positive attitudes about learning.

12. Students were excited and turned on to learning and interacting with each other.
13. Students gained more confidence in themselves.
14. Students seemed glad to help each other learn.

Faculty from both Friar Tuck and the other PDS schools believed that their participation in the PDS program enhanced their empowerment most along the collegiality dimension and the least in the area of decision making. Collegiality is critical to the creation of a school climate that is ripe for reform. PreK-12 teachers (cooperating teachers and others) indicated that they talked more with one another, were more willing to assist other teachers, participated more in cooperative planning, and were more willing to share and work with peers to improve teaching and learning in their school.

CONCLUSIONS

Lessons learned regarding the emergence and enhancement of teacher empowerment in school university partnerships include the following:

Initial Commitment

In order for meaningful school reform and teacher empowerment to emerge in a timely fashion, it may be important for preK-12 practitioners to be involved in the initial planning of reform. Teachers should clearly understand the theory and concepts on which an initiative is built as well as the time and resource commitments that will be required.

Time Commitment

Schools and universities must work together to devise creative and feasible ways to set aside the time required for reform to flourish. This includes time for collaboration and time to build trust and rapport. Teachers may feel resentful and uncooperative when they perceive that the majority of the time is spent in uncompensated after-school hours, rather than during the work day.

Practitioners as Teacher Educators

Many preK-12 practitioners are pleased to take part in the

teacher education process by becoming mentors for student teachers. They feel that they have something special to offer student teachers, and welcome the stimulation of new ideas that can come from new inductees into the profession.

Early Work on School Improvement Planning

School improvement planning appears to be one of the program components most critical to cementing the commitment of preK-12 professionals to the PDS process. Beginning work on the school improvement plan early in the process appears to help teachers focus better on the school's teaching and learning needs right from the beginning of the reform effort.

Training for Mentors

For schools that have not been clinical sites prior to becoming a PDS, early training in practice teacher supervision, evaluation, coaching, and reflective mentoring may enable the cooperating teachers to gain confidence in the role of mentors.

Training PreK-12 Practitioners as Action-Researchers

Action research—whether individual, collaborative, or schoolwide—has the potential for improving the practice and health of a school. PreK-12 teachers and administrators may need training and support in research methodology during the initial year of the PDS in order to use it as a powerful tool for improving teaching and learning in their schools (Calhoun 1993). As noted by Nystrand (1991), the rationale for establishing professional development schools rests on the premise that university and school personnel have shared interests in the improvement of both schools and teacher education. Too often, school reform has been initiated from the point of view that university professors are the experts and preK-12 practitioners are the recipients of their expertise. The PDS movement communicates that, while university personnel do have expertise to offer in improving teaching and learning in schools, preK-12 practitioners have expertise that enables the university to improve its teacher preparation program as well.

Table 7.1

Mentoring Self-Efficacy: Item Percentage Agreement by School			
Item	Friar Tuck	Comparison	X^2
Stem: As a result of my school's participation in the PDS program, I . . .			
Am a better role model for practice teachers.	69	73	0.22
Am better able to assist practice teachers.	53	72	3.67*
Have increased interest in helping practice teachers.	50	75	6.99*
Have more confidence in my ability to supervise and evaluate practice teachers.	56	72	2.59
Am more sensitive to the problems and stress experienced by practice teachers.	74	79	0.24
Can better coach others in skill development.	56	66	0.87
Recognize the need to improve my skills in working with practice teachers.	63	64	0.02

* $p < .05$.
Friar Tuck $\underline{n}=32$. Comparison $\underline{n}=82$.

Table 7.2

Collegiality: Item Percentage Agreement by School

Item	Friar Tuck	Comparison	X^2
Stem: As a result of my school's participation in the PDS program, I . . .			
Talk more with other teachers.	69	62	0.42
Am more willing to assist other teachers who may be experiencing problems.	72	72	0.00
Participate in more cooperative planning with other teachers.	75	67	0.68*
Am more willing to share and work with peers and evaluate practice teachers.	78	74	0.23

* p <.05.
Friar Tuck n=32. Comparison n=82.

Table 7.3

Teaching Self-Efficacy: Item Percentage Agreement by School			
Item	Friar Tuck	Comparison	X^2
Stem: As a result of my school's participation in the PDS program, I . . .			
Am more aware of the influence I can have in improving teaching and learning.	79	78	0.00
Have more influence in contributing to the success of others.	66	56	0.98
Have increased interest in helping practice teachers.	50	75	6.99*
Am more confident about my ability to work as an equal partner with university personnel in preparing new teachers.	66	74	0.88
Have increased my sense of professionalism.	72	68	0.14
Have increased confidence as a professional.	81	73	0.87

* $p < .05$.
Friar Tuck $n=32$. Comparison $n=82$.

Table 7.4

Professional Knowledge: Item Percentage Agreement by School

Item	Friar Tuck	Comparison	X^2
Stem: As a result of my school's participation in the PDS program, I . . .			
Am more knowledgeable about good and poor teaching practices.	69	73	0.22
Am more confident about my ability to help or teach students who are at risk of school failure.	74	51	4.86*
Have new insights into personality factors and their influences on teaching.	62	68	0.37
Have clarified my own beliefs about teaching.	56	62	0.29
Have used more cooperative problem-solving strategies.	69	65	0.11
Am more aware of individual styles of teaching.	75	75	0.00

*p <.05.
Friar Tuck n=32. Comparison n=82.

REFERENCES

Calhoun, E. F. 1993. "Action Research: Three Approaches." *Educational Leadership*, 51(2): 62-65.

Chambers, M. and B. Olmstead. 1971. "Teacher Corps and Portal Schools." *Portal Schools*, 1(1): 2-8.

Fay, C. 1992. "Empowerment Through Leadership: In the Teacher's Voice." In *Teachers as Leaders: Evolving Roles* (pp. 57-90). Edited by C. Livingston. Washington, D.C.: NEA Professional Library.

Foster, W. 1992. "Restructuring Schools." In *Encyclopedia of Education Research* (6th ed.), (Vol. 3, pp. 1108-1113). Edited by M. C. Alkin. New York: Macmillan Publishing Company.

Maeroff, G. 1988. "A Blueprint for Empowering Teachers." *Phi Delta Kappan,* 69: 472-477.

Morris, V. G. and J. A. Nunnery. 1993. *Teacher Empowerment in a Professional Development School Collaborative: Pilot Assessment* (Technical Report No. 931101). Memphis, Tenn.: Center for Research in Educational Policy, Memphis State University.

Morris, V. G., J. A. Nunnery, J. Scipio, J. Knight, M. Gopalakrishnan, and R. Rinehart. 1994. *A Case Study of Teacher Empowerment in a Professional Development School* (Technical Report No. 940101). Memphis, Tenn.: Center for Research in Educational Policy, Memphis State University.

Nystrand, R. O. 1991. *Professional Development Schools: Toward a New Relationship for Schools and Universities* (Trends and Issues Paper No. 3). Washington, D.C.: ERIC Clearinghouse on Teacher Education.

Romanish, B. 1991. *Empowering Teachers: Restructuring Schools for the 21st Century.* New York: University Press of America.

Stallings, J. A. and T. Kowalski. 1990. "Research on Professional

Development Schools." In *Handbook of Research on Teacher Education* (pp. 251-263). Edited by W. R. Houston. New York: Macmillan Publishing Company.

Wellins, R. S., W. C. Byham, and J. M. Wilson. 1991. *Empowered Teams: Creating Self-Directed Work Groups That Improve Quality, Productivity, and Participation.* San Francisco, Calif.: Jossey-Bass Publishers.

Yonemura, M. 1987. "Reflections on Teacher Empowerment and Teacher Education." In *Teachers, Teaching and Teacher Education* (pp. 276-283). Edited by M. Okazawa-Rey. Cambridge, Mass.: Harvard Educational Review.

Chapter 8

THE ROLE OF EVALUATION

by Mary Lee Hall, Lucindia Chance, Tom Rakes

If we are going to improve teacher preparation, what could be more crucial than the way we evaluate student teachers and the programs that train them? Evaluation helps students develop their teaching skills by pinpointing the areas where their performance is satisfactory and where it needs improvement. Evaluation helps teacher training institutions determine whether they are providing the sorts of experiences that prepare teachers to perform according to the highest standards of the profession. This chapter explores the role of evaluation in professional development schools, from new ways we've initiated to evaluate student teachers to how the sites themselves are evaluated.

EVALUATING STUDENT TEACHERS

Student teaching evaluation serves two major purposes. It seeks to nurture students in developing professional educational dispositions and skills, while determining how prepared they are to become teachers. A less acknowledged purpose of evaluation is to help future teachers understand the state-approved evaluation model so that they will have some knowledge of how they will be evaluated as licensed teachers.

With these purposes in mind, during the summer of 1991, representatives from local school systems, the State Department of Education, and the University of Memphis College of Education developed a new evaluation instrument known as the student teaching evaluation folder. The folder focused evaluation on six major domains of competency: planning, teaching strategies, evaluation, classroom management, leadership, and communication (Tennessee State Department of Education 1988). An updated version called the Framework for Evaluation and Professional Growth was adopted in 1995 (Tennessee State Department of Education) and focuses on six domains: planning, teaching strategies, assessment and evaluation, learning environment, professional growth, and communication. The process provides an opportunity for the cooperating teacher and university supervisor to rate the student teacher on two separate occasions in two progress reports and a final evaluation, which is a team effort. (See Appendix.)

A major distinction made in professional development schools is in the roles played by the cooperating teacher and university supervisor. Later in this chapter, we discuss the way in which cooperating teachers assume more responsibility for student teacher evaluation than in traditional schools.

The student teaching evaluation folder is considered a formative evaluation instrument. Schwebel et al. (1992) describe formative evaluation as taking place when the university liaison and the cooperating teacher advise but do not grade the student teacher. Through the use of questions or direct comments, or a combination of both, the mentors indicate ways in which the student teacher can be more effective. The aim is to promote the student teacher's development as a professional (p. 80). The instrument is also developmental, reflecting the designed growth and development of the student teacher throughout the placement. It provides adequate space for the university liaison and the cooperating teacher to comment on strengths observed in the classroom and to make specific suggestions for teacher improvement.

The evaluation process involves the cooperating teacher and the university liaison in post-conferences with the student teacher after three formal observations (indicated as Progress Reports One and Two and Final Evaluation in the folder). During the final evaluation, the mentors make a joint decision as to the final grade of pass, fail, or an IP (in progress) for the student teacher. If the student teacher receives an IP, the mentors determine how many weeks of the student teaching experience must be repeated before growth and development are considered adequate for passing. The student teacher may repeat only part of the placement of the total fifteen weeks in another placement.

The student teacher also has an opportunity for self-evaluation and receives direction from the university liaison about when to accomplish it. A journal guide is provided to help student teachers to reflect upon and analyze their teaching experience. The guide has a prescribed format. For example, during the weeks they are assuming full responsibility for the classroom, student teachers are asked to discuss good and bad lesson plans and to think critically about why the lesson was successful or unsuccessful. Group meetings with other student teachers and the university liaison are also a standard part of the self-evaluaton process.

Requirements for Student Teachers

Student teachers are placed in two different settings for the semester, one a placement of eight weeks and the other of seven weeks. These two placements (directed to licensure area) are designed to provide the student teacher with varied experiences. For example, a secondary licensure (grades 7-12) provides an opportunity for the student teacher to teach at the junior high and high school level. During the eight week placement, the student teacher is evaluated formally three times using the student teaching evaluation folder. Likewise, during the seven week placement, two formal evaluations are completed (Progress Report Two and the Final Evaluation).

Student teachers must complete four observations of other experienced teachers during the eight week placement and three observations during the seven week placement. These seven observations add a dimension to the student teaching experience by: (1) increasing knowledge of roles that librarians and music, art, and special education teachers play in the school; (2) offering a look at different teaching styles; and (3) enhancing involvement with many classroom teachers.

A KEY DISTINCTION IN ROLES

The same student teaching evaluation folder is used in regular school sites as is used in the professional development schools. However, the roles of the cooperating teacher and the university supervisor (or liaison) are quite different. In regular school sites, the university supervisor is not involved in inservice or group meetings but is still viewed as the primary evaluator of the student teacher. In professional development schools, the university liaison is involved in weekly meetings with student teachers but is not considered the primary evaluator. The cooperating teacher takes the lead in the evaluation process. The university liaison in a PDS uses the student teaching evaluation folder, but does not typically sit in the classroom for an hour formally observing a complete lesson. Instead, a snapshot evaluation is substituted.

Snapshot Evaluation

The snapshot evaluation instrument was developed by the Center for Research in Educational Policy at the University of Memphis (1990) and is officially called the Elementary Classroom Observation Measure. It is a modified version of a procedure called "walk-through evaluation" that was first used by school administrators during the early 1980s, and has more recently been used to evaluate the effectiveness of federally funded programs for at-risk learners (Chance and Rakes 1993). Demographic categories in the instrument provide for: (1) a drawing of the classroom, (2) a checklist of the resources available in the classroom, and (3) statistics on the physical environment and classroom appearance. The substance of the instrument is contained in two pages that use a five-minute observation coding system for nine unannounced visits to the classroom during the eight and seven week placement. The university liaison uses this instrument to record behaviors exhibited by the student teacher, other adults, and students in the classroom. The university liaison spends no more than five minutes during each of the nine visits and may never enter the room, but completes the instrument from the doorway. A sample of the coding sheet appears in Table 8.1.

Cooperating teachers in professional development schools have received training as mentors and, in that role, are much more important in the evaluation process. Schon (1988) describes supervision by cooperating teachers as a research activity. The cooperating teacher attempts to help the student teacher create meaning out of a problematic teaching situation. Both cooperating teacher and student teacher become researchers who reflect on teaching styles and strategies drawn from their existing base of examples, images, understandings, and actions.

Professional development schools and the concept of evaluation may constitute the first steps in building an empirical base for assuring that student teaching is a major contributor to the growth and development of teachers. In the past, student teaching evolved from practice, tradition, or as a matter of convenience (Guyton and McIntyre 1990).

EVALUATING SCHOOL IMPROVEMENT PLANS

Professional development schools are involved not only in evaluation of future teachers and improvement of school sites, but also in evaluation of the process itself. Focus groups and surveys developed by the Center for Research in Educational Policy in alliance with the Teacher Education Initiative of NEA (1994) have been given over the past five years (1995-2000) to gather information about how effective the professional development schools process is preparing future teachers. The research is also gathering information about the effectiveness of the partnership between the PDS and the university, use of technology, equity and diversity, teaching and learning, leadership roles, evaluation and dissemination, and internal and external systemic change.

University liaisons now meet regularly with cooperating teachers and student teachers to receive feedback. Weekly meetings with student teachers and cooperating teachers throughout the semester provide ongoing evaluation of the process and elicit specific problems they have encountered. Insights gained by sharing experiences and problems are enhanced because solutions are discussed in a group. The university liaison is the facilitator of group meetings.

University liaisons also visit regularly with the school administrators to evaluate not only the student teaching process, but to determine other faculty needs and training. A major focus of training over the past two years has been mentoring and peer coaching training for new teachers who were not involved in the original training when the school site first became a professional development school.

Evaluation at the university level also includes feedback sessions with student teachers. These take place at the end of each semester, with graduate and undergraduate student teachers attending on different days. The assistant dean of teacher education and the student teaching placement coordinator conduct the session, which begins with a written feedback instrument to be filled out by each student teacher. One of the questions is specific for professional development schools and asks student teachers to indicate whether they were in a PDS for one placement. If the answer is "yes," the student answers open-ended questions about the strengths and weaknesses of the PDS process, with specific reference to the differing roles of the university liaison and the cooperating teacher and the weekly meetings.

Annual evaluation of the professional development school program began during spring 1994 when university liaisons attended a meeting to discuss the PDS process. This informal discussion centered on what happened in PDS sites during the first year, and the liaisons learned from one another as they compared and evaluated activities at the different school sites. Plans were developed for the coming year, with strong emphasis placed on all PDS sites working as teams to share information.

A meeting of faculty members and administrators from PDS schools followed soon after. It began with each participant filling out a detailed survey, or Progress Evaluation. (See Table 8.2.)

Feedback from the sessions was analyzed for use by the professional development schools. The feedback indicated an overall satisfaction with the PDS concept, and all administrators and teachers wanted to continue for the next school year. Concern about weak areas of student teaching (Question 2), such as classroom management, led teachers to a commitment to working together to correct the deficits. Overall, PDS staff and faculty rated university support and liaison support as excellent. Both teachers and administrators felt that working with student teachers under the PDS umbrella was more favorable than working under more traditional arrangements. Evaluation through the Teacher Education Initiative surveys and focus groups has replaced the use of the instrument in Table 8.2.

CONCLUSIONS

In order to provide optimal teacher education for both student and inservice teachers, evaluation must be a key part of the entire collaborative effort between preK-12 schools and the university. Student teachers must receive structured feedback on how they measure up to high standards of professional practice. As PreK-12 teachers become primary mentors and evaluators of student teachers, the veteran teachers have an opportunity to share and reflect constructively on their own experience and expertise.

Table 8.1

Student Behaviors

TEACHER DIRECTED

Attention-Interest/Focus
Almost 100% foc.	① ② ③ ④ ⑤ ⑥ ⑦ ⑧ ⑨
75% are focused	① ② ③ ④ ⑤ ⑥ ⑦ ⑧ ⑨
50% are focused	① ② ③ ④ ⑤ ⑥ ⑦ ⑧ ⑨
25% are focused	① ② ③ ④ ⑤ ⑥ ⑦ ⑧ ⑨
Close to 0% foc.	① ② ③ ④ ⑤ ⑥ ⑦ ⑧ ⑨

Resources in Use
	① ② ③ ④ ⑤ ⑥ ⑦ ⑧ ⑨
Textbook	① ② ③ ④ ⑤ ⑥ ⑦ ⑧ ⑨
Story Book	① ② ③ ④ ⑤ ⑥ ⑦ ⑧ ⑨
Reference Book	① ② ③ ④ ⑤ ⑥ ⑦ ⑧ ⑨
Newspaper/Mag.	① ② ③ ④ ⑤ ⑥ ⑦ ⑧ ⑨

INDEPENDENT (STUDENT DIRECTED)

Attention-Interest/Focus
Almost 100% foc.	① ② ③ ④ ⑤ ⑥ ⑦ ⑧ ⑨
75% are focused	① ② ③ ④ ⑤ ⑥ ⑦ ⑧ ⑨
50% are focused	① ② ③ ④ ⑤ ⑥ ⑦ ⑧ ⑨
25% are focused	① ② ③ ④ ⑤ ⑥ ⑦ ⑧ ⑨
Close to 0% foc.	① ② ③ ④ ⑤ ⑥ ⑦ ⑧ ⑨

Resources in Use
	① ② ③ ④ ⑤ ⑥ ⑦ ⑧ ⑨
Textbook	① ② ③ ④ ⑤ ⑥ ⑦ ⑧ ⑨
Story Book	① ② ③ ④ ⑤ ⑥ ⑦ ⑧ ⑨
Reference Book	① ② ③ ④ ⑤ ⑥ ⑦ ⑧ ⑨
Newspaper/Mag.	① ② ③ ④ ⑤ ⑥ ⑦ ⑧ ⑨

Table 8.2

Professional Development Schools (PDS) Progress Evaluation

Check One: ___ **Principal** ___ **Teacher** ___ **Other** ___

	Poor				Excellent
1. The overall quality of the practice teachers in my school.	1	2	3	4	5
2. Rate the quality of practice teachers' knowledge or ability related to:					
– content	1	2	3	4	5
– unit and lesson planning	1	2	3	4	5
– instructional skills	1	2	3	4	5
– ability to work with all students	1	2	3	4	5
– ability to work with at-risk students	1	2	3	4	5
– classroom management skills	1	2	3	4	5
– ability to work with other teachers/staff.	1	2	3	4	5
3. Rate the overall university support for implementing PDS.	1	2	3	4	5
4. Rate the overall quality of university support in the following areas:					
– helping teachers be better mentors/supervisors	1	2	3	4	5
– keeping everyone informed	1	2	3	4	5
– providing needed supervisory materials	1	2	3	4	5
– demonstrating instructional techniques.	1	2	3	4	5
5. My understanding of the PDS concept.	1	2	3	4	5
6. How does working with practice teachers under PDS compare with working with student teachers under other arrangements with which you are familiar? (circle one).	Favorably Unfavorably				
7. I would like my school to continue being a PDS (circle one).	Yes				No

8. Strengths of PDS (write on back if necessary).

9. Areas needing improvement (write on back if necessary).

REFERENCES

Center for Research in Educational Policy. 1990. *Elementary Classroom Observation Measure.* Memphis, Tenn.: The University of Memphis.

Chance, L. H. and T. R. Rakes. 1993. "Differentiated Evaluation in Professional Development Schools: An Alternative Paradigm for Preservice Teacher Education." Unpublished manuscript.

Grossman, P. L. and N. S. Brantigan. 1992. "The Teacher as Teacher Educator: New Roles in Professional Development Schools." *Kappa Delta Pi Record,* 28 R(4): 116-120.

Guyton, E. and D. J. McIntryre. 1990. "Student Teaching and School Experiences." In *Handbook of Research on Teacher Education* (pp. 504-534). Edited by W. R. Houston, M. Haberman, and J. Sikula. New York: The Macmillan Co.

Kleinsasser, R. 1992. "Practice Teacher Evaluation." Unpublished manuscript.

Schon, D. A. 1984. "Coaching Reflective Teaching." In *Reflection in Teacher Education.* Edited by P. Grimmett and G. Ericksonis. NY: Teachers College Press.

Schwebel, A. I., B. L. Schewebel, C. R. Schwebel, and M. Schwebel. 1992. *The Student Teacher's Handbook* (2nd ed.). Hillsdale, N.J.: Lawrence Erlbaum Associates.

Chapter 9

CULTURAL CHANGES AT THE SCHOOL AND THE UNIVERSITY

by Vivian Gunn Morris, Marty M. Harrison, Judith N. Byrd, Dorothy Robinson

If preK-12 schools and universities are to enter into a true partnership, certain changes within the two cultures must take place to facilitate the new collaborative behaviors. This chapter focuses on the process of creating professional development schools by examining some of these essential changes—including changes in roles, relationships, and responsibilities—that are taking place at the professional development schools (PDS) at the University of Memphis and its 15 preK-12 sites. The chapter concludes with a look at those barriers that get in the way of a true partnership and the lessons we learned from our professional development school (PDS) model that might apply elsewhere. Sources of data for this chapter include naturalistic observations, focus group interviews, individual interviews at ten PDS sites over a two-year period, and findings from a survey of teacher perceptions administered at Friar Tuck Elementary School, an inner city PDS. The survey is an adapted version of one used by Berry and Catoe (1994) in a similar study.

PERCEPTIONS ABOUT TEACHING AND LEARNING

Building a PDS partnership means defying tradition at the preK-12 sites and the university in hopes that you will improve teaching and learning at both sites. If the perceptions of those involved in both places are accurate, we have made progress toward that goal. Our surveys show that participants in our PDS believe we have improved the student teaching experience and have provided the means for inservice teachers to expand their roles and change the way they teach. Nearly 75 percent of the responding teachers at Friar Tuck Elementary

School felt that the student teacher experiences at their school were more powerful and useful than traditional experiences at regular clinical sites. (See Table 9.1.) Very significantly, 100 percent (n=24) of the responding teachers thought student teachers at their school received sufficient support in learning how to teach. The roles of the preK-12 practitioners had evolved so that they were clearly seeing themselves as teacher educators in addition to being teachers of the young children in their classrooms.

Moreover, the combined efforts of the university liaison and the cooperating teacher appeared to provide the support needed to enable student teachers to become competent professionals. Approximately 96 percent of the Friar Tuck teachers believed that teachers at their school (1) had more responsibility for mentoring student teachers than teachers in nonPDSs and (2) received sufficient support in learning how to mentor student teachers. However, only 50 percent indicated that teachers had sufficient resources and time for their mentoring responsibilities.

When asked specifically about their roles (see Table 9.2), 96 percent of the teachers at Friar Tuck Elementary reported that teachers had taken on new roles and responsibilities in teacher education, while 88 percent felt that teachers had taken on research opportunities in partnership with university faculty. When it came to preK-12 involvement in university teaching, however, the results were more mixed. While a few teachers had served as guest lecturers in university classes, only 46 percent of the teachers indicated that Friar Tuck teachers were active in teaching college courses. Fifty-four percent of the teachers noted that university professors were taking on more responsibility in teaching public school classes, while fully 83 percent felt that their teachers and university professors worked together to plan and conduct school inservice programs.

In a follow study (Morris et al. 1998), Friar Tuck Elementary teachers were included in the responses of 211 teachers from eight schools in our partnership that asked teachers to list the benefits derived from mentoring student teachers. Veteran teachers noted that they:

- learned new ideas
- found opportunities to reflect on and evaluate their own teaching practices
- had opportunities to observe other teachers

Table 9.1

Practice Teaching in PDSs		
Friar Tuck School	**Faculty (n=24)**	
Survey Items	**% Disagree (Resp. 1, 2)**	**% Agree (Resp. 3, 4)**
In my school, practice teacher (or intern) experiences are more powerful and useful than the traditional practice teaching experiences.	25.2	74.8
As a result of our PDS efforts, teacher inservice has been more powerful and useful than traditional inservice.	33.4	68.6
In my school, practice teachers receive sufficient support in learning how to teach.	00.0	100.0
My school's teachers have more responsibility in mentoring prospective teachers than teachers in other schools.	4.2	95.6
In my school, teachers receive sufficient support in learning how to mentor practice teachers.	4.2	95.6
My school's teachers have sufficient resources and time for their mentoring responsibilities.	49.0	50.1

Note: For the above survey, respondents were to rate their level of agreement (or disagreement) statements circling the appropriate number along the continuum: 1=strongly disagree, 2=disagree, 3=agree, 4=strongly agree.

Table 9.2

Roles and Responsibilities in PDSs

Friar Tuck School Survey Items	Faculty (n=24)	
	% Disagree (Resp. 1, 2)	% Agree (Resp. 3, 4)
As part of our PDS efforts, teachers have taken on new roles and responsibilities in teacher education.	4.2	95.8
As part of our PDS efforts, teachers have taken on research opportunities in partnership with university faculty.	12.8	87.5
My school's teachers are active in teaching college level courses.	54.2	45.8
University professors are taking on more responsibility in teaching public school classes.	45.8	54.2
My school's teachers and university professors work together to plan and conduct school in-service programs.	16.7	83.3

Note: For the above survey, respondents were to rate their level of agreement (or disagreement) with the statements by circling the appropriate number along the continuum: 1=strongly disagree, 2=disagree, 3=agree, 4=strongly agree.

- improved classroom management skills
- had increased energy for teaching
- experienced satisfaction in assisting future teachers.

These findings make the case for supervision of student teachers as an important source of professional development for veteran teachers.

How Teachers Have Changed

During the first year of the PDS program, a great deal of inservice training time was devoted to learning about new teaching strategies that were identified in the school improvement plan. From our survey, the results of these efforts appear to have paid off. (See Table 9.3.) Fully 71 percent of the teachers indicated they had changed their conception of teaching, and 91 percent had changed the way they taught since their school became a PDS. Additionally, 66 percent of Friar Tuck teachers felt that teachers had changed the way they interacted and worked with their students, while 83 percent indicated that teachers had changed their conception of what needs to be known in order to teach. Seventy-one percent of the teachers at Friar Tuck believed that teachers at their school had changed their commitment to teaching and to the work of the PDS program. Very significantly, 96 percent of the teachers felt that—as a result of PDS efforts—teachers at Friar Tuck had changed their reflections upon their own practices.

The primary motive for preK-12 schools to join a PDS partnership is to improve teaching and learning at their schools, and, for many teachers, this implied making changes in the curriculum. However, only 46 percent of the responding teachers at Friar Tuck felt that the content of the curriculum had changed as a result of becoming a PDS. An earlier study (Morris et al. 1994) reported that teachers felt stymied when it came to making curricula changes because of district and state level mandates.

Table 9.3

Teaching and Learning in PDSs

Friar Tuck School	Faculty (n=24)	
As a result of PDS efforts at my school, teachers have changed:	% Disagree (Resp. 1, 2)	% Agree (Resp. 3, 4)
The content of the curriculum.	54.2	45.8
Their conception of teaching.	29.2	70.8
The way they teach.	9.0	91.0
Their conception of collegial work.	29.2	70.8
The way they interact and work with their students.	25.0	66.4
Their conception of what needs to be known in order to teach.	16.7	83.3
Their commitment to teaching and/or to the work of the PDS.	29.2	70.8
Their reflections upon their own practices.	4.2	95.8

Note: For the above survey, respondents were to rate their level of agreement (or disagreement) with the statements by circling the appropriate number along the continuum: 1=strongly disagree, 2=disagree, 3=agree, 4=strongly agree.

EXPANDED ROLES

Of all the role changes in a first-year PDS, the one identified by school faculty as having the greatest impact was the change from traditional university supervision of student teachers to supervision by a team consisting of classroom (cooperating) teacher, university liaison, administrator, and student teacher. Other team efforts that signaled role and responsibility changes for preK-12 teachers included making curriculum changes at the PDS sites, making recommendations for improving the teacher education program at the university, grant writing, conducting research, making presentations at professional meetings, and writing articles for professional publications. Elsewhere in this book, authors have discussed these team efforts, so we don't intend to explore each one in this chapter. We will briefly review progress made in three areas: grant writing, research, and preparation of presentations.

Grant Writing

Grant writing was activated very early in the PDS. Teachers viewed this process as one that would enable them to implement curricula changes identified in the school improvement plan and to acquire needed resources to implement plans that were impossible to do within the regular school budget. The process began with grant writing workshops conducted for PDS faculties at each school site by the Director of Development for the College of Education. The grant writing process followed in a fairly sequential pattern at PDS sites: (1) university liaison writing grant for the preK-12 school (based on goals and objectives identified in the school improvement plan), with input from the PDS faculty; (2) university liaison writing grant, with input from a faculty grant writing committee; (3) school grant committee writing grant, with university liaison serving as consultant; and (4) joint grant writing by a team including all schools from the partnership and university faculty.

By the end of the second year of the collaborative, PDS sites had been awarded grants to implement: (1) a whole language program, (2) a nongraded K-2 program, (3) a conflict resolution initiative, (4) a K-6 literacy program involving parents, (5) a parent efficacy study, and (6) a program designed to expand the experiential base for at-risk inner city children through field trip experiences in the local community.

However, these grant awards included only a small percentage of the proposals that were actually written and submitted for funding. Also, in the second year of the PDS program, a grant writing team composed of school personnel from several professional development schools and university liaisons wrote a proposal for the entire partnership to improve science and mathematics instruction through the use of technology. This collaborative effort served to enhance collegiality and mutual respect among faculty across PDS sites and with other university liaisons. Beginning with the third year of the project, teacher teams have been successful in receiving grant awards in a variety of areas including technology, science, and mathematics instruction and parental involvement. Teacher teams write the grants, while the liaison serves as a consultant—the original intent.

Shared Research and Professional Presentations

Because the work of the PDS is developmental, it is critical that PDS partnerships document the process of change and implementation from the very beginning (Robinson and Darling-Hammond 1994). In their review of research on PDSs, Stallings and Kowalski (1990) emphasized the critical need for longitudinal evaluations and experiments that explore the new PDS models in undergraduate, graduate, elementary, and secondary preparation and credentialing. They emphasized that research on this topic must be accomplished quickly so that the effectiveness of the PDS models can be validated before more traditional student teaching programs are eliminated.

With support from the Center for Research in Educational Policy in the College of Education, the PDS project at the University of Memphis began its research efforts to assess and evaluate the program at the beginning of implementation. Data from these studies helped to improve the program for the second year (Morris and Nunnery 1993; Morris et al. 1994). The research findings were shared with PDS faculties, which included their own recommendations for program improvement. For example, at Friar Tuck, the faculty worked together with the liaison throughout the year to decide how to best implement the suggested changes.

At Boysen Elementary, PDS teams conducted several action research projects, including the topics of whole language for kindergarten classes, inclusion, and conflict resolution in the classroom. The research teams included classroom teachers, the principal, student teachers, the university liaison, and other university faculty members. School-university teams from several professional development schools in the partnerships have made presentations at local and state professional meetings on their collaborative efforts. School-university teams also submitted articles for publication in professional journals, and submitted proposals for regional and national presentations for the 1994-95 academic year. This process of research, publications, and presentations has continued through the life of this project. (DeMeulle and Anderson 1994; Lowther and Morrison 1997; Lowther, Morrison, and Abraham 1997; Mahood, DeSimone, and Warner 1996; Mahood, Grannan, and Sparkman 1997; Mahood and Grannan 1997; Maxwell 1996; Morris, Branch, and Taylor 1995; Morris and Chance 1997; Morris, Chance, and Rakes 1996-97; Morris, Taylor, Knight, and Mogge 1998; Morris, Taylor, Nunnery, Burr-McNeal, and Knight 1997).

University Liaison and Faculty Rapport Building

There is more to changing the roles of participants in a professional development school than changing the scope of work they undertake. Clearly, the relationships that must develop are key to creating a culture where success can occur. One relationship that is particularly important is the one between the university liaison and preK-12 faculty. Rapport building between the two does not take place at all sites at the same time and does not ever take place among some liaisons and individual faculty members. In our model, it generally took the entire first year before university liaisons were accepted as equal partners by the majority of the preK-12 faculty members. Some liaisons who continued to work on this still had difficulty with it at the end of the second year. But, when acceptance occurs, it is worth all of the time, effort, tears, and frustration.

University liaisons tell moving, emotional, and very personal stories of the first time they felt truly accepted as a member of the preK-12 team. One university liaison reported her experience during the first year of the project:

Although all teachers attended the workshop sessions on a regular basis, some teachers exhibited their dissatisfaction by conducting loud second conversations during inservice meetings. The university liaison was made aware that some of the coldness and rudeness experienced during the first term was due to some of the teachers' anxiety associated with the amount of time spent in after-school, clinical professor training—a commitment they had not fully understood when they voted to become a professional development school.

However, by January, the beginning of the second term of the program, the distracting behavior subsided. This change in behavior appeared to be associated with a developing rapport with and trust in the university liaison. At the first meeting of the second term, the university liaisons made a statement to the teachers which referenced a local newspaper article: The longer I live here, the more I understand what it takes for you to get up to come to teach every morning. The teachers applauded. This appeared to be one of the events marking the turning point toward a more positive climate for inservice meetings (Morris et al. 1994, p. 28).

Disruptive teacher behavior at inservice meetings had virtually vanished by the beginning of the second year of the PDS project. Perhaps one of the contributing changes in this behavior was the scheduling of most of the meetings with inservice (and preservice) teachers during the school day rather than after school. Among the six sites, a pattern emerged during the process of university liaison and faculty rapport building, as shown in Figure 9.1. This sequential pattern begins with mutual respect and understanding between the university liaison and the principal and progresses to universal acceptance of each other by university professors and preK-12 school faculty.

Figure 9.1
Stages of Development Between University Faculty And Pre K-12 Professionals

Stage 11   TOTAL UNIVERSITY FACULTY/TOTAL PRE K-12 FACULTY
Mutual Respect/Understanding/Acceptance

Stage 10   NONLIAISON UNIVERSITY FACULTY PRE K-12 FACULTY
Growing Acceptance

Stage 9   NONLIAISON UNIVERSITY FACULTY PRE K-12 FACULTY
Shared Roles/Professional Collaboration

Stage 8   NONLIAISON UNIVERSITY FACULTY PRE K-12 FACULTY
Limited Acceptance

Stage 7   UNIVERSITY LIAISON PRE K-12 FACULTY
Mutual Respect/Understanding/Acceptance

Stage 6   UNIVERSITY LIAISON PRE K-12 FACULTY
Growing Acceptance

Stage 5   UNIVERSITY LIAISON PRE K-12 FACULTY
Shared Roles/Professional Collaboration

Stage 4   UNIVERSITY LIAISON PRE K-12 PRINCIPAL
Perceived as Team by P-12 Faculty

Stage 3   UNIVERSITY LIAISON PRE K-12 FACULTY
Limited Acceptance

Stage 2   UNIVERSITY LIAISON PRE K-12 PRINCIPAL
Team Building/Joint Decision Making

Stage 1   UNIVERSITY LIAISON PRE K-12 PRINCIPAL
Mutual Respect/Understanding

CHANGES AT THE UNIVERSITY

In order for PDS collaborations to be successful, there must be commitment from top leadership in each organization. This commitment must be evidenced by providing the support and resources required to carry out the work of the partnership. One of the most critical resources is time away from the traditional work of each organization (Robinson and Darling-Hammond 1994).

We are fortunate in that the University of Memphis College of Education Dean, Nate Essex, has made a long-term commitment to the work of the partnership. Core funding for the PDS partnership came from the College of Education's regular budget. This fiscal commitment includes: (1) releasing university liaisons from teaching university courses to facilitate the work of the PDS at each site, (2) releasing other university professors on an as-needed basis to conduct inservice training at the PDS sites to support their school improvement plans, (3) providing duplicating services to support the work of the partnership, and (4) supporting travel needs for both school and university faculty to present papers at professional conferences reporting on research and the work of the PDS partnership.

Other changes that have taken place in the college as a result of the PDS project include: (1) university professors teaching students in preK-12 classes, (2) an increased number of preK-12 professionals from PDSs serving as guest lecturers for university classes, (3) an increased number of undergraduate method courses being taught at school sites, (4) university liaisons and other professors supervising M.A.T. (Masters of Arts in Teaching) theses and special projects related to topics or problems identified by PDS classroom teachers, and (5) university liaisons organizing on-site graduate courses for PDS faculty related to needs identified in their school improvement plans.

BARRIERS TO CHANGE

The traditional reward system for tenure and promotion at universities has generally placed high priority on research and publications. While service to preK-12 schools has been encouraged, it has been a low priority item. In addition, because the work of professional development schools is often a labor intensive venture and can be very time consuming, both senior and junior faculty members sometimes choose not to participate in this important collaboration with preK-12 schools. The work of the PDS would take them away from the work that is more highly valued by the university reward system.

At the University of Memphis, both the college dean and the president of the university have communicated clearly their commitment to the importance of service to preK-12 schools through the allocation of faculty and money resources to the PDS partnerships and related collaboratives with city and county schools. A university-wide committee was convened to rewrite the present tenure and promotion policies. As expected, the committee redefined the meaning of scholarship for the university with a higher priority placed on teaching and service to preK-12 schools. While several senior faculty members had already decided to serve as university liaisons in the third year of the project, it was expected that the new tenure and promotion policies would be an added stimulus for encouraging more professors to make long-term commitments to the work of the PDS partnership. As noted in Chapter 4, it appears that this goal was achieved.

For preK-12 professionals, the major barrier to making changes in the schools is time: time for planning, for mentoring student teachers, for reflecting on practice, for grant writing, for inservice training, and for collaborating with peers and university partners. Other barriers may include a comfort level with present conditions in the school environment and an initial mistrust of university professors who have come to help.

The superintendents in each of the five school districts that comprise our PDS partnership have demonstrated their commitment to the collaborative by accepting clusters of student teachers at each site, allocating inservice time to the work of the partnership, allowing flexible use of school hours for task force meetings, providing release time for teachers to visit innovative classrooms at local and out-of-town schools, and providing resources for travel to conferences related to needs identified in the school improvement plans. While these resources have been of critical importance to the work of the partnership, the lack of time remains an obstacle to implementing the agenda agreed on by the partners. Teachers at Friar Tuck (Morris et al. 1994) identified three other barriers that slowed the progress of their work: shortage of money to support the action plans and activities found in the school improvement plan, lack of parental involvement, and large class size.

LESSONS LEARNED

Findings from studies conducted over the life of the PDS partnership indicated that culture changes are taking place at both the schools and the university as a result of the work of the PDS partnership. Both preK-12 professionals and university professors are taking on new roles and developing new relationships with partners in the collaborative. However, further changes are needed in order to meet the common goals of the partnership in a timely fashion. Discussed below are some of the lessons learned that should help effect the changes needed for continued growth and development of the collaborative. These lessons may also be useful to other organizations that are planning to establish similar partnerships.

Short placements should be extended. Inducting new teachers into the profession through the student teaching process is a major part of the work of the PDS. Although one goal of PDSs is to have all student teachers complete their placements within one school, during the first year many student teachers had separate placements in two schools—a ten-week placement in a PDS and a five-week placement at a regular school site. We found the five-week placement too short to complete the mentoring deemed necessary for a high quality experience, especially if the placements are at two different schools. The ten-week placements in a PDS seemed to result in the student teacher doing better work and identifying more closely with the faculty. However, if both the ten-week and five-week placements are at the same PDS, with placements at two different grade levels, students have the advantage of extended opportunities to develop good relationships with the school faculty.

Completing the entire student teaching experience at one school need not be limiting if students have been exposed to a variety of clinical experiences through their methods courses prior to student teaching. Feedback from student teachers, cooperating teachers and support faculty, and university liaisons indicate that this pattern resulted in a higher quality growth experience for student teachers. Student teachers came to school earlier, were more involved in inservice training, and they attended regular meetings of the faculty and functions of the parent-teacher organizations. If the partnership does not have enough professional development schools in which to place all student teachers, universities may consider equalizing the weeks in each placement or extending the short placement, which would increase the total number of weeks in the student teaching experience. Placement in both PDSs and regular clinical sites have been changed to eight weeks at the first site and seven weeks at the second.

Student teachers make contributions and have fresh ideas. Cooperating teachers at one inner city school site in our PDS model reported that the presence of student teachers in their classrooms exposed the children to something they were unaccustomed to and that for the first time their students were talking about attending the university. Cooperating teachers indicated that: (1) their work with student teachers enhanced their supervisory and teaching skills, (2) they valued the opportunity to discuss information received in the PDS inservice workshops with student teachers, (3) they were stimulated by the new ideas about teaching and learning that student teachers brought to the classroom environment, (4) they believed that having two teachers working as a team in the classroom enhanced their students' opportunities for growth and development, and (5) they felt they were uniquely equipped to prepare student teachers to work with children from diverse backgrounds (Morris et al. 1994; Morris et al. 1998).

Not all classroom teachers can be or should be cooperating teachers in PDSs. Some classroom teachers seem especially suited to be mentors for student teachers, while others who have the desire but lack the skills can profit from training in clinical supervision, coaching, and reflective mentoring. Many good classroom teachers have neither the skills nor the desire to be effective cooperating teachers. Assigning student teachers to the latter can result in poor quality experiences for the classroom students, the student teachers, and the cooperating teacher, and can wreak havoc in the school and in the teacher education program. When the principal and university liaison work as a team to create compatible placements, such disasters can usually be avoided.

Every PDS is not the same. PreK-12 schools in a university partnership may have a common vision and goals that provide a framework for the work of the collaborative. However, each school site is unique, with different students, teachers, and communities that have differing needs. This will be reflected in the school improvement or development plan that guides the work of each site. As a result, schools in the same partnership often look very different from one another.

Risk-taking can be worthwhile. The work of the PDS is developmental and constantly changing to meet the needs of all stakeholders in the partnership. While the collaborative should begin with a clear vision and common goals (and the desired end in mind), the road map is incomplete. This means that this community of learners must be willing to take risks and to be flexible, knowing that mistakes will be made. However, making mistakes can be valuable if lessons are learned from them.

The PDS concept takes time and the process is slow. Time is required for collaboration and building mutual trust and respect among partners in PDSs. Much of the first year may be needed to create the rapport required for a successful long-term partnership. Our experience indicates that effective university liaisons have usually been accepted as members of the preK-12 school community by the end of the first year.

School-university faculty joint research, publications, and presentations provide additional opportunities for reflection on practice. We have found our collaborative efforts in planning and conducting research projects, presentations at conferences, and publications to be cathartic experiences. Even though we interact on a regular basis, these experiences provide important new information about the impact or results of our work together. These events provide additional data that enable the partnership to assess the work of the PDSs and plan for future growth and development.

CONCLUSIONS

When preK-12 schools and a university seek to form a true partnership, a culture must be created that supports the development of this new relationship. Essential to that culture is a common vision and clearly stated goals for the work of the two institutions together. Also essential is an atmosphere of mutual respect and trust. These conditions will greatly aid participants in the difficult process of changing roles, responsibilities, and relationships with one another. Our experience over the last seven years indicates that, while the process is slow and there are many barriers, lasting and positive culture changes can take place both at the university and the preK-12 schools as a result of the work of the PDS partnership.

REFERENCES

Berry, B. and S. Catoe. 1994. "Creating Professional Development Schools: Policy and Practice in South Carolina's PDS Initiatives." In *Professional Development Schools: Schools for Developing a Profession* (pp.176-201). Edited by L. Darling-Hammond. New York: Teachers College Press.

Carnegie Forum on Education and the Economy, Task Force on Teaching as a Profession. 1986. *A Nation Prepared: Teachers for the 21st Century.* New York: Carnegie Forum on Education and the Economy, Task Force on Teaching as a Profession.

Demuelle, L. and R. S. Anderson. December 1994. "Building Collaborative Cultures Through Constructed Knowing." Paper presented at the annual meeting of the Confluent Education Special Interest Group, American Educational Research Association, Santa Barbara, Calif.

Holmes Group. 1986. *Tomorrow's Teachers: A Report of the Holmes Group.* East Lansing, Mich.: Holmes Group.

Lowther, D. L. and G. R. Morrison. February 1997. "Project SMART: Changing One Classroom at a Time." Paper presented at the Association for Educational Communication and Technology National Conference, Albuquerque, N. Mex.

Lowther, D. L., G. R. Morrison, and K. Abraham. March 1997. "Professional Development for Successful Computer Integration." Paper presented at the 1997 Tennessee Educational Technology Conference, Nashville, Tenn.

Mahood, R. M., E. A. DeSimone, and J. M. Warner, Sr. March 1996. "Are Preservice Teachers Perceived as 'Real Teachers' in a Professional Development School?" *National Social Perspective Journal.* Proceedings of the March 1996 National Social Science Association, Las Vegas Conference, 11:2: 87-101.

Mahood, R. M, J. W. Grannan, with M. F. Sparkman, 1997. "Cooperative Learning: Think-Group-Share Activities in a Secondary English Composition/Literature Classroom." *National Social Science Perspectives Journal.* Proceedings of the National Social Science Association, April 1997, Las Vegas Conference, 11:2: 87-101.

Mahood, R. M. and J. W. Grannan. November 1997. "Mentor Support Systems for the Pre-Service Teachers in a Professional Development School (PDS)." Presentation made at the National Social Science Conference, San Antonio National Conference.

Maxwell, S. A. 1996. "The Pattern Quilt Metaphor: Revisiting the PDS Concept." *Contemporary Education,* 47(4): 196-199.

Morris, V. G., E. Branch, S. I. Taylor, 1995. *Improving the Literacy Skills of K-6 At-risk Students Through Parental Involvement: Final Report on Student Success Program at Frayser Elementary School, 1994-95.* Memphis, Tenn.: College of Education, The University of Memphis. (ERIC Document Reproduction Service No. ED 386 448).

Morris, V. G. and L. Chance. 1997. "Customized Professional Development for In-service Teachers in a School-University Partnership." *British Journal of In-service Education,* 23 (3): 335-348.

Morris, V. G., L. Chance, and T. A. Rakes. 1996-97. "School Improvement Planning: A Critical Key in Urban School Reform." *National Forum of Teacher Education Journal,* 6 (2): 26-36.

Morris, V. G., S. I. Taylor, J. Knight, and K. Mogge. February, 1998. "Mentor-Teaching As a Source of Professional Development in a School-University Partnership." Paper presented at the 79th Annual Meeting of the Association of Teacher Educators, Dallas, Tex.

Morris, V. G., S. I. Taylor, J. A. Nunnery, B. Burr-McNeal, and J. Knight. 1997. *Parent Efficacy, Teacher Efficacy, and Parent Involvement in Professional Development Schools: Research Report for Frayser Elementary School.* Memphis, Tenn.: College of Education, The University of Memphis. (ERIC Document Reproduction Service No. ED 399 219).

Morris, V. G. and J. A. Nunnery. 1993. *Teacher Empowerment in a Professional Development School Collaborative: Pilot Assessment* (Technical Report No. 931101). Memphis, Tenn.: Center for Research in Educational Policy, Memphis State University.

Morris, V. G., J. A. Nunnery, J. Scipio, J. Knight, M. Gopalakrishnan, and R. Rinehart. 1994. *A Case Study of Teacher Empowerment in a Professional Development School* (Technical Report No. 940101). Memphis, Tenn.: Center for Research in Educational Policy, Memphis State University.

Robinson, S. and L. Darling-Hammond. 1994. "Change for Collaboration and Collaboration for Change: Transforming Teaching Through School-University Partnerships." In *Professional Development Schools: Schools for Developing a Profession* (pp. 203-219). Edited by L. Darling-Hammond. New York: Teachers College Press.

Stallings, J. A. and T. Kowalski. 1990. "Research on Professional Development Schools." In *Handbook of Research on Teacher Education* (pp. 252-263). Edited by W. R. Houston. New York: Macmillan Publishing Company.

APPENDIX

STUDENT TEACHING EVALUATION FORM

Student Teacher _____ **School** _____

Subject and Grade _____ **Date/Time/Period** _____

Please rate the student's performance as a student teacher by checking each category at some point on the scale. In addition, write a concise statement which explains and supplements your ratings. Use a different form for each progress report.

1. Needs Improvement   2. Satisfactory   3. Excellent

Progress Report One ___ **Progress Report Two** ___ **Final** ___

PLANNING

___(CT) ___(US)   ___(CT) ___(US)   ___(Final Evaluation)

   A. Establishes appropriate instructional goals and objectives

   B. Develops timely and appropriate lessons to match goals and objectives

TEACHING STRATEGIES

___(CT) ___(US)   ___(CT) ___(US)   ___(Final Evaluation)

   A. Demonstrates understanding of the central concepts, tools of inquiry, and structures of the discipline(s) taught and provides students access to this information through experiences which make the subject matter meaningful

   B. Demonstrates an understanding of and uses a variety of instructional strategies to encourage students' development of critical and creative thinking, problem solving, and performance skills

   C. Uses an understanding of both the students and the subject matter to create a learning environment that encourages active engagement in learning, positive intellectual interactions and student ownership of the learning

ASSESSMENT & EVALUATION

___(CT) ___(US)   ___(CT) ___(US)___(Final Evaluation)

A. Uses appropriate assessment strategies and instruments to obtain information about students and their ongoing progress and uses this information to make instructional decisions

B. Communicates student status and progress to students, their parents, and appropriate others

C. Reflects on teaching practice by evaluating continually the effects of instruction

D. Evaluates student performance and determines the amount of progress

LEARNING ENVIRONMENT

___(CT) ___(US)   ___(CT) ___(US)___(Final Evaluation)

A. Creates a learning climate that supports the development of student abilities

B. Manages classroom resources effectively

PROFESSIONAL GROWTH

___(CT) ___(US)   ___(CT) ___(US)___(Final Evaluation)

A. Collaborates with colleagues and appropriate others

B. Performs professional responsibilities

COMMUNICATION

___(CT) ___(US)   ___(CT) ___(US)___(Final Evaluation)

A. Uses appropriate verbal and nonverbal techniques to communicate effectively with students, parents, and appropriate others

B. Writes clearly and correctly

PROGRESS REPORT ONE

COMMENTS   DATE _____

PROGRESS REPORT TWO

COMMENTS   DATE _____

FINAL EVALUATION

COMMENTS   DATE _____

ACKNOWLEDGMENTS

Acknowledgments

Collaboration between America's schools and universities is contingent upon both groups accepting a new belief system and being willing to discontinue business as usual and accept a new paradigm. This paradigm requires the dynamic leadership of visionaries unafraid of change and the challenges it brings. Since this book would not be possible without their vision and action, the editor would like to acknowledge such leaders. The preK-12 teachers and university professors, school principals, and university department chairs and the professional development school coordinator and the dean and school superintendents are the real heroes of this effort. Without their tireless work, sincere enthusiasm, boundless energy, and countless hours of time, the PDSs at the University of Memphis would not exist.

Special recognition for visionary leadership goes to the superintendents of the five school systems involved in the initial collaborative partnership and to the dean of the college:

Dr. Nathan Essex, Dean, College of Education

Dr. Gerry House, Superintendent, Memphis City Schools

Dr. James Anderson, Superintendent, Shelby County Schools

Dr. Carol Kulpa, Superintendent, Catholic Dioceses of Memphis

Dr. Dwight Hedge, Superintendent, Dyer County Schools, and

Dr. Elsie Danley, Superintendent, Jackson-Madison County Schools.

Acknowledgments, praise, and leadership recognition go to the principals and teachers of the 13 professional development schools and to the department faculty and leadership at the university.

Many school and university leadership changes have occurred during the 7-year history of the University of Memphis PDSs. With each change, the PDSs were impacted with a slight refocusing. However the theme of simultaneous renewal and focus on student achievement/improvement, served as the stabilizing force. The following are current professional development schools with their school and university leadership.

Neddy Brookshaw, Principal, Bishop Byrne High School, Memphis, Tennessee

Dr. Lirah Sabir, Principal, Caldwell Elementary, Memphis, Tennessee

Susan Copeland, Interim Director, Campus School, The University of Memphis, Memphis, Tennessee

Dr. Murphysteen Campbell, Interim Principal, Coleman Elementary School, Memphis, Tennessee

Willie Willett, Principal, Dunn Elementary School, Memphis, Tennessee

Kelly Council, Principal, Dyer County Elementary School, Dyersburg, Tennessee

Barbara Miller, Principal, Frayser Elementary School, Memphis, Tennessee

Dr. Gwendolyn Boyd, Director, Lipman Early Childhood Center, The University of Memphis, Memphis, Tennessee

Marilyn Ingram, Principal, Newberry Elementary School, Memphis, Tennessee

Larry Winegarden, Principal, Raleigh-Egypt Middle School, Memphis, Tennessee

David Carlisle, Principal, Riverdale Elementary School, Germantown, Tennessee

Lois Williams, Principal, Ross Elementary School, Memphis, Tennessee

Frank Bratcher, Principal, Whitehall Elementary School, Jackson, Tennessee

University initiatives that require significant change in the academy must have advocates that are tireless and dedicated. Without the leadership of Vivian Morris, Director of Professional Development Schools and Mary Lee Hall, Coordinator of Field Experiences, the PDS initiative at the University would not have survived. Both of these dedicated professionals continued to push for full implementation of the PDS concept and legitimated its existence with research throughout its implementation.

Due to lack of space, it is impossible to list the names of all the teachers, university liaisons, curriculum coordinators, and others who were, and continue to be, instrumental in the daily operations that have resulted in successful professional development schools. I would, however, like to acknowledge these groups and their professional leadership and enthusiasm in implementing and sustaining the program. Without these dedicated professionals, professional development schools would not exist.

I would also like to extend special acknowledgment to the Center for Innovation, Teacher Education Initiative of the National Education Association. Dr. Charles Williams and Sylvia Seidel's leadership in the Center reflects a commitment to preparing teacher leaders for the twenty-first century. This leadership has resulted in a national initiative of recognition for restructured teacher education programs, a seven-site longitudinal evaluation of these programs and a national collaborative to serve in a major leadership role for the professional development school movement. It has been and continues to be a pleasure to work with these two visionary leaders and with the six other sites recognized by the NEA as leaders in this school-university partnership movement. The sites recognized by the National Education Association and included in this initiative are:

> George Mason University, Fairfax, Virginia
>
> Montclair State University, Montclair, New Jersey
>
> Texas A&M University, College Station, Texas
>
> University of South Carolina, Charleston, South Carolina
>
> University of Memphis, Memphis, Tennessee
>
> University of Southern Maine, Portland, Maine
>
> University of Wyoming, Laramie, Wyoming.

Professional development schools, as reflected through the chapters of this volume, operationalize the somewhat modified proverb "it takes a whole professional education community to successfully educate teacher education candidates and the children of this nation."

Lucindia Chance
Editor

PROFESSIONAL DEVELOPMENT SCHOOLS

Bishop Byrne High School
1475 East Shelby Drive
Memphis, TN 38116
(901) 346-3060
Principal, Neddy Brookshaw
Liaison, Ramona Mahood

Caldwell Elementary
230 Henry Avenue
Memphis, TN 38107,
(901) 579-3200
Principal, Dr. Lirah Sabir
Liaison, Dr. Elnora Roane

Campus School
The University of Memphis
Memphis, TN 38152
(901) 678-2285
Interim Director, Susan Copeland
Liaison, Dr. Janie Knight

Coleman Elementary School
3210 Raleigh-Millington Rd.
Memphis, TN 38128
(901) 385-4306
Interim Principal,
Dr. Murphysteen Campbell
Liaison, Dr. Robert Bolding

Dunn Elementary School
1500 Dunn Avenue
Memphis, TN 38106
(901) 775-7816
Principal, Willie Willett
Liaison, Lillian Whitney

Dyer City Central Elementary
Hornbrook Street
Dyersburg, TN 38024
(901) 385-1337
Principal, Kelly Council
Liaison, Dr. J.F. Crabtree

Frayser Elementary School
1602 Dellwood
Memphis, TN 38118
(901) 357-3840
Principal, Barbara Miller
Liaison, Dr. Nancy Easley

Lipman Early Childhood Center
The University of Memphis
Memphis, TN 38152
(901) 678-2120
Director, Dr. Gwendolyn Boyd
Liaison, Dr. Satomi Taylor

Newberry Elementary School
5540 Newberry
Memphis, TN 38138
(901) 385-4306
Principal, Marilyn Ingram
Liaison, Dr. Elnora Roane

Raleigh-Egypt Middle School
4215 Alice Ann Drive
Memphis, TN 38128
(901) 385-4141
Principal, Larry Winegarden
Liaison, Bonnie Cummings

Riverdale Elementary School
7391 Neshoba
Germantown, TN 38138
(901) 756-2300
Principal, David Carlisle
Liaison, Dr. Mabel Himel

Ross Elementary School
4890 Ross Road
Memphis, TN 38115
(901) 369-1990
Principal, Lois Williams

Whitehall Elementary School
532 Whitehall
Jackson, TN 38301
(901) 427-6396
Principal, Frank Bratcher
Liaison, Dr. J. F. Crabtree

Professional development schools : combining school improvement and teacher preparation